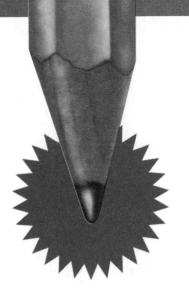

GRAMMARWORK

1

English Exercises
in Context

PAMELA PETERSON BREYER

Longman

Acquisition Editor: Nancy Leonhardt
Manager of Development Services: Louisa B. Hellegers
Development Editors: Carol Callahan and Gina Protano
Editorial Consultant: John Chapman

Director of Production and Manufacturing: David Riccardi
Editorial Production/Design Manager: Dominick Mosco

Production Coordinator: Ray Keating
Page Composition, Production, and Realia: Lido Graphics
Cover Design Coordinator: Merle Krumper
Cover Design: Marianne Frasco
Electronic Art: Peter Ticola and Todd Ware
Interior Design: Patrice Fodero
Interior Art: Lane Gregory and Dorothea Sierra

Printed in the United States of America

19 20 21 22 23 V001 15 14 13 12 11

ISBN 0-13-340241-X

Printed on Recycled Paper

To my mother, Dorothy Peterson

CONTENTS

Introduction   **xi**

Verb to *Be*

Affirmative Statement

Contracted Forms: **I'm** Susan Burns.   1
I, You, He, She

Subject Pronouns   **He's** from Spain.   2
He, She

Possessive Adjectives: **My** first name is Susan.   3

My, Your, His, Her

Possessive of Singular Nouns   Susan is **Dorothy's** daughter   4, 5

Adjectives   Is her hair long or short? It's **long.**   6, 7

Articles *A* and *An*   She's **an** artist.   8, 9

Word Order with Adjectives   He's a **good** doctor.   10

Articles *A* and *An* with Adjectives   It's **an** easy job.   11

Word Order with Articles and Adjectives   Athens is **an interesting** city.   12

Review: Verb *To Be*, Possessive Adjectives **She's** an interior decorator.   13

Affirmative Statements   Louise and Raymond **are** from Paris.   14

Subject Pronouns and Contractions   **They're** Spanish.   15

Possessive Adjectives   **Their** native language is Spanish.   16

Regular Noun Plurals   They're **electricians.**   17

Regular Noun Plurals with Adjectives   We're good **actors**.   18

Yes-No Questions   **Is he** a good lawyer?   19

                                           Is she from Paris?   20

Negative Statements   He **isn't** here right now.   21

Negative and Affirmative Statements   John and Carmen **aren't** married.   22

Negative and Affirmative Short Answers   Is Louise a hairdresser? **Yes, she is**.   23, 24

Word Order with Statements and   **Quebec is a beautiful city.**   25
Questions

It with Time   **It's** nine o'clock.   26, 27

Adverbs of Frequency   He's **never** late to work.   28

Money and Numbers   Fifteen and No/100-Dollars   29

Regular Noun Plurals: *-s, -es*	Two **hairbrushes** for $5.45	30, 31
Regular Noun Plurals: *-s, -es, -ies*	**Cherries** are $1.99 a pound.	32
Irregular Noun Plurals	Shoes for **men**	33
Demonstrative Pronouns *This* and *That*	**That's** my camera.	34
Demonstrative Pronouns *These* and *Those*	Are **these** your keys?	35
That and *Those* Before Nouns	**Those** shoes are on sale.	36
These and *Those* Before Nouns	**These** dresses are beautiful.	37
Questions with *How Much*	**How much** are they?	38
Questions with *Who, What, Where*	**Who** is his teacher?	39
	Where is his class?	40
Review: Long and Short Answers and Verb *To Be*	**I'm** in Math 1A this semester.	41
Review: Verb *To Be*	My husband and I **are** artists.	42
Prepositions of Place: *In* and *On*	The knife is **on** the counter.	43

There Is and There Are

Affirmative Statements *There is* and *There are*	**There's** a fireplace in the living room.	44, 45
Articles *A* and *The*	There's **a** refrigerator in the kitchen.	46
Yes-No Questions	**Is there a** dishwasher in the kitchen?	47
Word Order with *Yes-No* Questions	Is there a fire detector in the apartment?	48
Negative and Affirmative Short Answers	Is there a window in the kitchen? **Yes, there is.**	49
Some with Countable and Uncountable Nouns	There's **some** meat on the plates.	50, 51
A with Countable Nouns and *Some* with Uncountable Nouns	There's **some** salt on the table.	52
Any with Negative Statements	There isn't **any** water in the pitchers.	53
Countable and Uncountable Nouns	a lemon eggs milk	54
Some and *Any* with Affirmative and Negative Statements	There are **some** eggs in the refrigerator. There isn't **any** meat.	55
Any with *Yes-No* Questions	Is there **any** soda?	56
Review: *There Is, There Are,* Prepositions, Articles, Word Order	**There's** a bookcase in the classroom.	57

Present Continuous

Affirmative Statements	A little boy **is eating** an ice cream cone.	58, 59
	She**'s wearing** a suit.	60
Spelling	He's sit**ting** in a chair.	61
Negative Statements	They **aren't** watching television.	62
Negative and Affirmative Statements	She **isn't** wearing a hat.	63
Yes-No Questions	**Is she** sleeping?	64
Negative and Affirmative Short Answers	Is the girl winning the game? **Yes, she is.**	65
Questions with *What*	**What's he doing?**	66
It with Weather	**It**'s raining in London.	67
Review: Present Continuous	In Athens, people **are** probably **working**.	68

Future with *Going To*

Affirmative Statements	He's **going to play** tennis.	69
	Susan **is going to work** in the yard.	70, 71
Negative and Affirmative Short Answers	Is she going to play tennis? **Yes, she is.**	72
Negative Statements	Leonard and Dorothy **aren't** going to wash the car.	73
	They **aren't** going to run tomorrow.	74
Questions with *Who, When, What Time*	**Who** is she going to have dinner with?	75
Review: Future with *Going To*	They're **going to take** a lot of pictures.	76

Present Continuous

Contrast: Future with *Going To* vs. Present Continuous	She's **going to play** tennis. She's **playing** tennis.	77
Contrast: Future with Going to, Present Continuous, Verb *To Be*	It**'s going to rain** tomorrow. It**'s raining** now.	78

Imperative

Prepositions of Place: *Next To, Across From, Between, On*	The post office is **across from** the police station.	79
Affirmative Statements	**Walk** to the corner.	80
Negative Statements	**Don't stop** here.	81

Simple Present

Affirmative Statements	She **works** in a hospital.	82
Spelling: *-s, -es, -ies*	After dinner, he **relaxes** on the couch.	83
Prepositions of Time: *In* and *At*	She usually goes to bed **at** midnight.	84
Adverbs of Frequency	He **never** drinks wine.	85
Affirmative Statements: *Have* and *Has*	I **have** a headache.	86
	You **have** a big family.	87
Affirmative Statements: *-s, -es*	She **loves** animals.	88, 89
	She **has** two full-time jobs.	90
Yes-No Questions	**Do** you **have** any brothers and sisters?	91
	Does he **get** at 9:00?	92
Negative and Affirmative Short Answers	Do they live in Los Angeles? **Yes, they do**.	93
Negative Statements	They **don't work** in the daytime.	94
	She **doesn't make** a lot of money.	95
Object Pronouns: *Them* and *It*	Who has my keys? I have **them**.	96
Object Pronouns	Please help **me**.	97
Object and Subject Pronouns	**I** see him, but he doesn't see **me**.	98
Prepositions of Place: *In, On, At*	She lives **on** Park Avenue.	99
Questions with *Where*	**Where** in Los Angeles do you live?	100
Questions with *What* and *Where*	**What** does he do?	101
Review: Simple Present	Christa's mother **takes** care of their son.	102
Contrast: Present vs. Present Continuous	Chuck and Christa **watch** TV every night. They**'re watching** TV now.	103
Contrast: Adverbs of Frequency with the Present	It's **usually** cool in the fall.	104
Contrast: Present vs. Present Continuous	It always **snows** in the winter. It**'s snowing** now.	105

Can

Affirmative Statements	She **can play** the piano very well.	106
Negative Statements	She **can't** dance.	107
Too and *Very*	These shoes are **too** narrow.	108
	It's **too** heavy.	109
Negative and Affirmative Short Answers	Can you lift the couch? **No, I can't**.	110, 111

| Yes-No Questions | Can you move the box? **Can you** move it? | 112 |
| Review: *Can* | I **can** ski but not very well. | 113 |

Past of Verb *To Be*

Affirmative Statements	The beaches **were** beautiful.	114
Negative Statements	The weather **wasn't** nice.	115
Yes-No Questions	**Was it** sunny?	116
Negative and Affirmative Short Answers	Were Maria and Pedro at the movies? **No, they weren't.**	117
No Article with *Home, Church, School, Work*	We were at school.	118
Was Born and *Were Born*	I **was born** on June 28.	119
Prepositions of Time: *In* and *On*	Akira and I were born **in** June.	120

Past of Regular Verbs

Affirmative Statements	I **stayed** at home last Saturday night.	121
	She **studied** math in high school.	122, 123
Negative and Affirmative Short Answers	Did she sign the application? **No, she didn't.**	124, 125
Negative Statements	She **didn't use** a pen.	126
Negative and Affirmative Statements	He **didn't live** with his uncle. He **lived** with his brother.	127, 128
Questions with *When, Where, Who, What*	**When did** you **arrive** in the United States?	129
Questions with *When* and *How Long*	**How long** did he work for National Bank?	130
Review: Past, Past of *To Be*	At 11:30, Mohsen **watched** the late show on TV.	131
Contrast: Past, Present Continuous, Future with *Going To*	Yesterday he **was** in Miami. Tomorrow he's **going to fly** to Chicago.	132, 133
Contrast: Past, Present Continuous, Future with *Going To*	We**'re staying** at the Excelsior Hotel.	134

Appendix

135

Numbers, Days of the Week, Months of the Year

Answers to Exercises

136

INTRODUCTION

Recent studies have shown that students acquire and retain a new language more rapidly and efficiently when the structure and vocabulary of the language are presented in context; that is, when elements of a lesson, such as grammar and new lexicon, are tied together in some real and meaningful setting. Exercises that present material in such a situational context are referred to as contextualized exercises.

GrammarWork is a series of four contextualized exercise books for students of written English. These books may be used as major texts or as supplementary material, depending on whether a course is nonintensive or intensive. Each exercise in each book presents, as a unit, vocabulary relating to a particular context and structures that are appropriate to that context.

Book One is intended for the beginner: the student enrolled in a first-level English course who has had some exposure to the language. Book Two continues with beginners' material, proceeding from first-level to second-level work. Book Three is designed for the intermediate student, and Book Four contains material appropriate to high-intermediate levels.

The books are organized into grammatical units (i.e., the Verb *To Be*, the Present Continuous, the Simple Present). Each unit has a variety of exercises with practice in small increments. Most units include more than one exercise on key grammar points, in order to give students ample and varied practice. Also included in each unit are review exercises and periodic tense contrast exercises, usually located at the end of the unit.

The pages in each book are, for the most part, divided into three sections:
a. an examination of the structure to be presented (**Grammar**);
b. exercises that enable the student to manipulate that new structure in a contextual setting (**Practice**); and
c. a culminating exercise activity in which the student uses the material in the exercise by applying it to some personal, real-life situation (**Make It Work**).

The **Grammar** section shows the student how to use the structure to be practiced, with diagrams and arrows that should be self-explanatory. Notes of explanation are supplied only when the grammar rule cannot be illustrated clearly.

The **Practice** section consists of a contextualized exercise, usually a page in length and always self-contained; if a context is three pages instead of one, the exercise will be self-contained within those three pages. Thus the teacher can select any exercise or group of exercises he or she considers appropriate for a particular class, lesson, or given time. The teacher can choose to utilize all the exercises in the order presented. The exercises have been arranged in ascending order of difficulty, with structures generally considered to be the easiest for most students presented first.

The exercises are self-contained in that they have been designed for written practice without necessarily being preceded by an introductory teacher's presentation. Since grammatical diagrams have been included and the new vocabulary is usually illustrated or defined, students can work independently, either at home or in class—in pairs or as a group. When students work together in pairs or in groups in the classroom, they should be encouraged to help each other; the teacher can assist by circulating from pair to pair or group to group, guiding and correcting.

The **Make It Work** section enables students to apply what they have been practicing to freer, and sometimes more natural, situations. The activity usually contains a picture cue, a fill-in dialogue, or questions to answer. The purpose of the **Make It Work** section is to provide the student with as real-life a setting as possible.

The perforated answer key can be used by either the student or the teacher. The teacher may choose to withhold the answers on some occasions; on other occasions, the students may use the answer key for self-correction.

I'M SUSAN BURNS.

Contracted Forms: *I, You, He, She*

Verb *To Be*

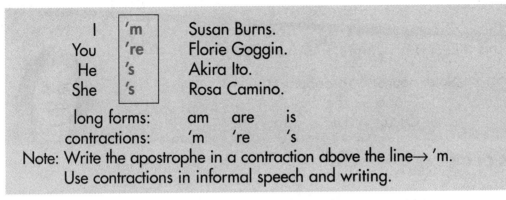

I	**'m**	Susan Burns.
You	**'re**	Florie Goggin.
He	**'s**	Akira Ito.
She	**'s**	Rosa Camino.

long forms: am   are   is

contractions: 'm   're   's

Note: Write the apostrophe in a contraction above the line→ 'm.
Use contractions in informal speech and writing.

PRACTICE

Fill in the blanks with the correct contraction.

1. He   *'s*   Loi Van Ha.

2. She _____ Anna Thanos.

3. You _____ Rafael Moreno.

4. She _____ Gloria Sánchez.

5. I _____ Louise Du Lac.

6. You _____ Akira Ito.

7. She _____ Marie Du Lac.

8. He _____ Carlo Alba.

9. You _____ Julia Santos.

10. I _____ Chang Wu.

11. He _____ Mohsen Abdul.

12. You _____ Oscar Sánchez.

MAKE IT WORK

Introduce yourself to a classmate.

■ Hi, _____

☐ (It's) nice to meet you.

1

HE'S FROM SPAIN.

Subject Pronouns: *He, She*

Verb *To Be*

This is Oscar.	**He's**	from Spain.
This is Gloria.	**She's**	from Spain.

Note: nouns   pronouns
Gloria = she
Oscar = he

PRACTICE

Make sentences with pronouns and contractions.

1. This is Loi. (Vietnam)   *He's from Vietnam.*

2. This is Anna. (Greece) _____

3. This is Rafael. (Colombia) _____

4. This is Carlo. (Italy) _____

5. This is Marie. (Canada) _____

6. This is Louise. (France) _____

7. This is Mohsen. (Egypt) _____

8. This is Akira. (Japan) _____

9. This is Julia. (Brazil) _____

10. This is Chang. (China) _____

MAKE IT WORK

Introduce two friends (a man and a woman) to each other.

This is_____. _____ from _____.

And this is_____. _____ from _____.

MY FIRST NAME IS SUSAN.

Possessive Adjectives: *My, Your, His, Her*

Verb *To Be*

I'm Susan.	**My**	name is Susan.
You're Bruce.	**Your**	name is Bruce.
He's Bruce.	**His**	name is Bruce.
She's Susan.	**Her**	name is Susan.

I'm Susan Jill Burns. My first name is Susan. My middle name is Jill. My last name is Burns. My full name is Susan Jill Burns.

P R A C T I C E

Fill in the blanks.

She's Dorothy Helen Peterson. 1. *Her first name is* _____ Dorothy.

2. _____ Helen.

3. _____ Peterson.

He's Leonard Peterson. 4. _____ Peterson.

5. _____ Leonard.

You're Brian Burns. 6. _____ Brian.

7. _____ Burns.

He's John Christopher Burns. 8. _____ John.

9. _____ Burns.

10. _____ Christopher.

She's Barbara Burns. 11. _____ Burns.

12. _____ Barbara.

MAKE IT WORK

Answer the questions.

What's your first name? _____

What's your middle name? _____

What's your last name? _____

What's your full name? _____

SUSAN IS DOROTHY'S DAUGHTER.

Possessive of Singular Nouns

Verb *To Be*

Leonard Dorothy

Diane Susan Bruce

Brian John Barbara

SUSAN IS DOROTHY'S DAUGHTER.

Susan is Dorothy	's	daughter.
Dorothy is Susan	's	mother.

Note: noun   possessive of noun
      Susan   Susan's

PRACTICE

Look at the picture on page 4. Then fill in the blanks with a possessive form.

1. Leonard is *Susan's* _____ father.

2. Dorothy is _____ mother.

3. Susan is _____ daughter.

4. Susan is also _____ daughter.

5. Bruce is _____ husband.

6. Susan is _____ wife.

7. Diane is _____ sister.

8. John is_____ son.

9. Barbara is _____ daughter.

10. Barbara is _____ sister.

11. Barbara is also_____ sister.

12. John is_____ brother.

13. Leonard is _____ grandfather.

14. Dorothy is _____ grandmother.

15. Diane is _____ aunt.

MAKE IT WORK

Fill in the blanks with the names of your family. Then tell about your family.

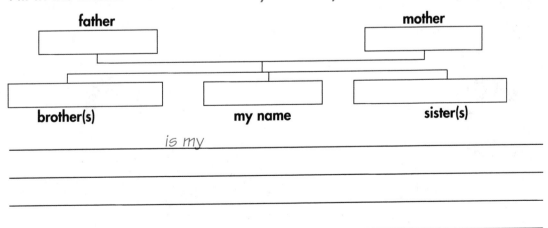

father

mother

brother(s)   my name   sister(s)

_____ *is my* _____

_____

_____

_____

IS HER HAIR LONG OR SHORT? IT'S LONG.

Adjectives

Verb *To Be*

Is she

heavy   or   thin?

tall   or   short?

old   or   young?

Is her hair

long   or   short?

curly   or   straight?

IS HER HAIR LONG OR SHORT? IT'S LONG.

Is Louise heavy or thin?   She's   thin.
Is her hair long or short?   It's   long.
Note: The word *hair* is singular.

Raymond   Paul   Louise

PRACTICE

Look at the picture above. Then answer the questions. Use contractions whenever possible.

1. Is Raymond tall or short?   _He's short._

2. Is he heavy or thin?   _____

3. Is he old or young?   _____

4. Is his hair long or short?   _____

5. Is his hair curly or straight?   _____

6. Is Louise heavy or thin?   _____

7. Is she tall or short?   _____

8. Is her hair long or short?   _____

9. Is her hair curly or straight?   _____

10. Is Paul old or young?   _____

11. Is he heavy or thin?   _____

12. Is he tall or short?   _____

MAKE IT WORK

Tell about yourself.

I'm   _____

My hair   _____

7

SHE'S AN ARTIST.

Articles *A* **and** *An*
Verb *To Be*

a	nurse	an	artist
a	student	an	electrician
a	lawyer	an	interior decorator
a	teacher	an	office manager
a	secretary	an	usher

Note: Use *an* before the vowel sounds *a, e, i, o,* and *u.*
Use *a* before all other sounds.

PRACTICE

Fill in the blanks with *a* or *an.*

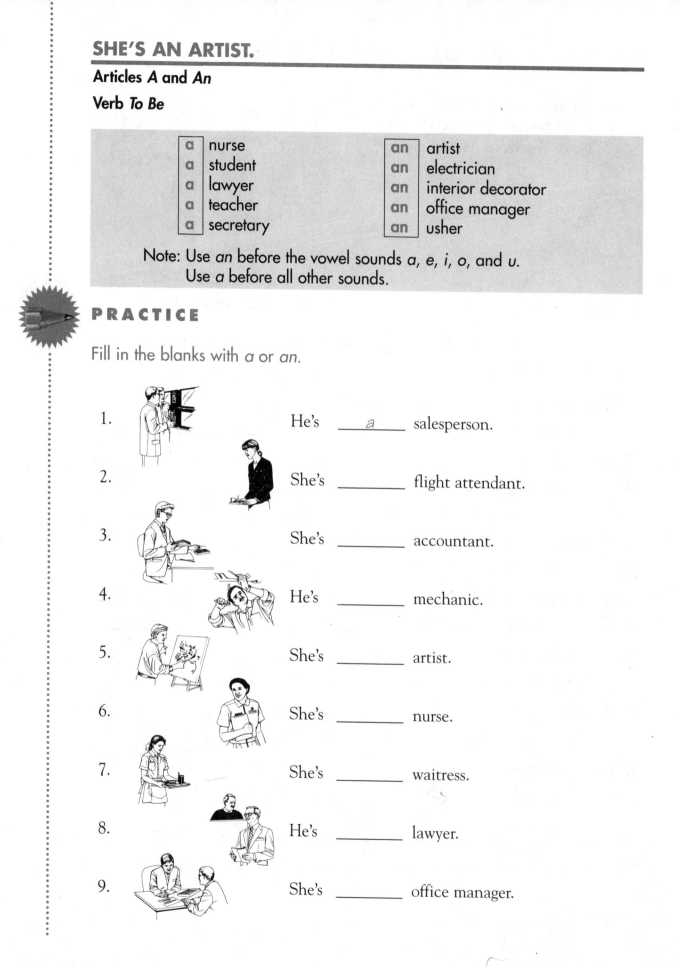

1. He's _____a_____ salesperson.

2. She's _____ flight attendant.

3. She's _____ accountant.

4. He's _____ mechanic.

5. She's _____ artist.

6. She's _____ nurse.

7. She's _____ waitress.

8. He's _____ lawyer.

9. She's _____ office manager.

SHE'S AN ARTIST.

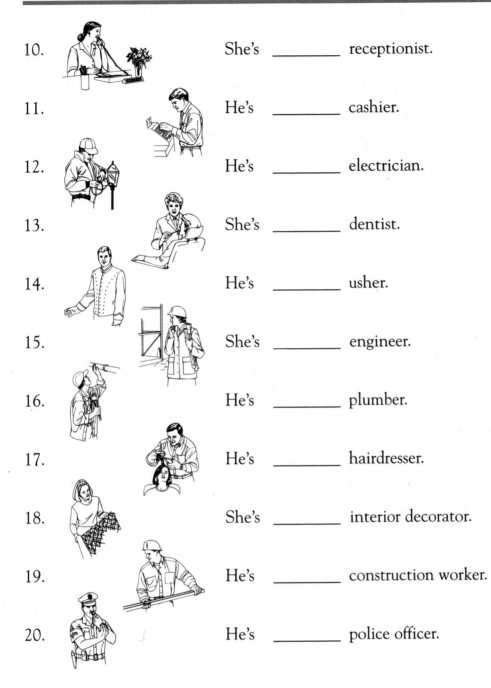

10. She's _____ receptionist.

11. He's _____ cashier.

12. He's _____ electrician.

13. She's _____ dentist.

14. He's _____ usher.

15. She's _____ engineer.

16. He's _____ plumber.

17. He's _____ hairdresser.

18. She's _____ interior decorator.

19. He's _____ construction worker.

20. He's _____ police officer.

MAKE IT WORK

Answer the question.

What's your occupation? _____

New Word: occupation = job

HE'S A GOOD DOCTOR.

Word Order with Adjectives
Verb *To Be*

	ADJECTIVE	NOUN
He's a		doctor.
He's a	good	doctor.

PRACTICE

Add the adjectives to the sentences.

1. He's a student. (good)   *He's a good student.*

2. She's a waitress (bad)   _____

3. She's a hairdresser. (busy)   _____

4. He's a teacher. (good)   _____

5. She's a nurse. (hardworking)   _____

6. He's a mechanic. (lazy)   _____

7. She's a secretary. (busy)   _____

8. He's a manager. (bad)   _____

9. She's a lawyer. (famous)   _____

10. He's a salesperson. (hardworking) _____

11. She's a receptionist. (friendly) _____

12. He's a doctor. (famous)   _____

MAKE IT WORK

Answer the question.

Are you a good student or a bad student? _____

_____

IT'S AN EASY JOB.

Articles *A* and *An* with Adjectives
Verb *To Be*

It's	a	job.	It's easy.
It's	an	easy job.	

PRACTICE

Combine the sentences.

1. It's a job. It's good.   *It's a good job.* _____
2. It's a job. It's easy.   _____
3. It's a job. It's difficult.   _____
4. It's a job. It's important.   _____
5. It's a job. It's interesting.   _____
6. It's a job. It's tiring.   _____
7. It's an occupation. It's boring.   _____
8. It's an occupation. It's exciting.   _____
9. It's an occupation. It's dangerous. _____
10. It's an occupation. It's excellent. _____
11. It's an occupation. It's terrible. _____
12. It's an occupation. It's stressful. _____

MAKE IT WORK

Look at the dialogue. Then answer the questions about yourself.

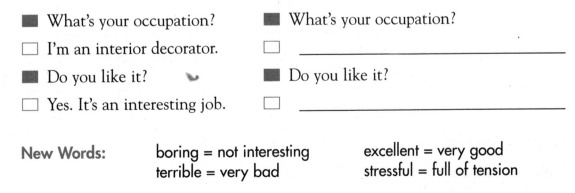

■ What's your occupation?

☐ I'm an interior decorator.

■ Do you like it?

☐ Yes. It's an interesting job.

■ What's your occupation?

☐ _____

■ Do you like it?

☐ _____

New Words: boring = not interesting   excellent = very good
                    terrible = very bad   stressful = full of tension

ATHENS IS AN INTERESTING CITY.

Word Order with Articles and Adjectives
Verb *To Be*

		ARTICLE	ADJECTIVE	NOUN
Tokyo	is	a	crowded	city.
		an	important	

PRACTICE

Look at the chart. Make some affirmative sentences. Then write them.

Cairo			famous	
New York			important	
Los Angeles			interesting	
London			modern	
Paris	is	a	old	city.
Tokyo		an	big	
Rome			exciting	
Madrid			beautiful	
Mexico City			expensive	
Athens			crowded	

1. *Cairo is an old city.*
2. _____
3. _____
4. _____
5. _____
6. _____
7. _____
8. _____

MAKE IT WORK

Tell about the city you are from.

I'm from _____. It's _____

_____

SHE'S AN INTERIOR DECORATOR.

Review: Verb *To Be*, Possessive Adjectives

PRACTICE

Read what Gloria Sanchez says about herself. Then rewrite the sentences. Tell about Gloria. Change *I* to *she* and *my* to *her*.

> My name is Gloria. My maiden name is Blanco. I'm married, and my last name is Sánchez. My husband is a dentist. My father is an accountant and my mother is a housewife. I'm an interior decorator. I'm also an ESL student. I'm from Madrid.

Her name is Gloria.

_____

_____

_____

_____

_____

_____

_____

_____

_____

MAKE IT WORK

Tell about yourself and your family.

_____

_____

_____

_____

New Word: maiden name = a woman's last name before she marries
ESL = English as a second language

LOUISE AND RAYMOND ARE FROM PARIS.

Affirmative Statements

Verb *To Be*

I	am	from Los Angeles.	My husband and I	are	from Los Angeles.
You	are	from Tokyo.	You and Akira	are	from Tokyo.
Louise	is	from Paris.	Louise and Raymond	are	from Paris.
Raymond	is	from Paris.			

PRACTICE

Fill in the blanks with *am are,* or *is.*

1. Oscar and Gloria _____are_____ from Spain.

2. Oscar _____ from Seville, and Gloria _____ from Madrid.

3. Bruce and I _____ from the United States.

4. I _____ from Los Angeles, and Bruce _____ from Los Angeles, too.

5. You and Akira _____ from Japan.

6. You _____ from Osaka, and Akira _____ from Tokyo.

7. Carlo and his wife _____ from Italy.

8. Carlo _____ from Rome, and his wife _____ from Naples.

9. Rafael and his wife _____ from Colombia.

10. His wife _____ from Santa Marta. Rafael _____ from Bogotá.

11. You and Mohsen _____ from Egypt.

12. Mohsen _____ from Cairo, and you _____ from Cairo, too.

MAKE IT WORK

Answer the questions.

Where are you from?_____

What country are your parents from? _____

What city is your father from? _____

What city is your mother from? _____

14

THEY'RE SPANISH.

Subject Pronouns and Contractions
Verb *To Be*

		country		nationality
Gloria	is	from Spain.	She's	Spanish.
Oscar	is	from Spain.	He's	Spanish.
Gloria and I	are	from Spain.	We're	Spanish.
Gloria and her husband	are	from Spain.	They're	Spanish.

Note: Nationalities are capitalized: **S**panish.

PRACTICE

Make sentences with contractions.

1. Loi is from Vietnam. (Vietnamese)　　*He's Vietnamese.*
2. Chang and Lee are from China. (Chinese) _____
3. Akira and I are from Japan. (Japanese) _____
4. Julia is from Brazil. (Brazilian) _____
5. Mohsen and I are from Egypt. (Egyptian) _____
6. Carlo is from Italy. (Italian) _____
7. Marie and her brother Paul are from Canada. (Canadian) _____
8. Rosa is from Mexico. (Mexican) _____
9. Rafael is from Colombia. (Colombian) _____
10. Dorothy is from England. (English) _____
11. Louise and I are from France. (French) _____
12. Leonard is from the United States. (American) _____
13. Gloria and Oscar are from Spain. (Spanish) _____
14. Anna and her sister are from Greece. (Greek) _____

MAKE IT WORK

Answer the question.

What's your nationality? _____

THEIR NATIVE LANGUAGE IS SPANISH.

Possessive Adjectives

Verb *To Be*

I'm	from Spain.	**My**	native language is Spanish.
You're	from Spain.	**Your**	native language is Spanish.
He's	from Mexico.	**His**	native language is Spanish.
She's	from Mexico.	**Her**	native language is Spanish.
We're	from Colombia.	**Our**	native language is Spanish.
You're	from Colombia.	**Your**	native language is Spanish.
They're	from the Peru.	**Their**	native language is Spanish.

Note: Languages are capitalized: **S**panish.

PRACTICE

Make sentences with possessive adjectives.

1. They're from China. (Chinese) *Their native language is Chinese.*
2. He's from Vietnam. (Vietnamese) _____
3. You're from Mexico. (Spanish) _____
4. She's from Spain. (Spanish) _____
5. He's from Colombia. (Spanish) _____
6. We're from England. (English) _____
7. I'm from the United States. (English) _____
8. You're from Italy. (Italian) _____
9. They're from France. (French) _____
10. I'm from Canada. (French) _____
11. We're from Japan. (Japanese) _____
12. She's from Greece. (Greek) _____

MAKE IT WORK

Answer the questions.

What's your native language? _____

What's your second language? _____

THEY'RE ELECTRICIANS.

Regular Noun Plurals

Verb *To Be*

> He's   an electrician.
> She's   an electrician.   **They're** electrician ⓢ .
>
> Note: Add *s* to form the plural: mechanic→mechanics   nurse→nurses
>   The plural form does not use the articles *a* and *an*.

PRACTICE

Make plural sentences.

1. He's an accountant. She's an accountant.   *They're accountants.*
2. She's a cashier. He's a cashier.   _____
3. She's a manager. He's a manager.   _____
4. He's a lawyer. She's a lawyer.   _____
5. She's an usher. He's an usher.   _____
6. He's an artist. She's an artist.   _____
7. He's a nurse. She's a nurse.   _____
8. She's a doctor. He's a doctor.   _____
9. He's a hairdresser. She's a hairdresser.   _____
10. He's an engineer. She's an engineer.   _____
11. She's a teacher. He's a teacher.   _____
12. He's a dentist. She's a dentist.   _____

MAKE IT WORK

Look at the pictures. Then answer the questions.

What does he do?

He's _____

What does she do?

_____

What do they do?

_____

WE'RE GOOD ACTORS.

Regular Noun Plurals with Adjectives

Verb *To Be*

I'm a good actor.	**We're**	good actors.
You're a hardworking nurse.	**You're**	hardworking nurses.
He's an experienced office manager.	**They're**	experienced office managers.
She's an excellent teacher.	**They're**	excellent teachers.
It's an interesting occupation.	**They're**	interesting occupations.

Note: Adjectives have no plural ending.

PRACTICE

Make plural sentences.

1. You're a good usher.   *You're good ushers.*

2. It's an interesting occupation.   _____

3. I'm an experienced engineer.   _____

4. It's a difficult job.   _____

5. You're a busy receptionist.   _____

6. He's a bad waiter.   _____

7. I'm a good cashier.   _____

8. You're an excellent hairdresser.   _____

9. It's an important job.   _____

10. He's a famous actor.   _____

11. She's an intelligent student.   _____

12. It's a stressful job.   _____

MAKE IT WORK

Fill in the blanks.

Tom Cruise and Kevin Costner _____ _____ actors.

18

IS HE A GOOD LAWYER?

Yes-No Questions

Verb *To Be*

He's a lawyer.	I'm a lawyer.
Is he a good lawyer?	Are you a good lawyer?
They're lawyers.	We're lawyers.
Are they good lawyers?	Are you good lawyers?

PRACTICE

Make questions. Add the word *good* to each question.

1. I'm a doctor.   *Are you a good doctor?*

2. We're accountants.   _____

3. He's a cashier.   _____

4. She's a hairdresser.   _____

5. I'm a secretary.   _____

6. She's a nurse.   _____

7. They're lawyers.   _____

8. We're electricians.   _____

9. He's a mechanic.   _____

10. We're doctors.   _____

11. I'm a dentist.   _____

12. They're interior decorators.   _____

                                   _____

MAKE IT WORK

REad the dialogue. Then fill in the blank.

■ I need a good mechanic.   ■ I need a good hairdresser.

☐ Loi Van Ha is a mechanic.   ☐ Louise Du Lac is a hairdresser.

■ Is he a good mechanic?   _____

☐ Yes. He's excellent.   ☐ Yes. She's excellent.

IS SHE FROM PARIS?

Yes-No Questions

Verb *To Be*

Louise is from France.	Louise and Raymond are from France.
Is she from Paris?	Are they from Paris?

PRACTICE

Make questions with pronouns.

1. Oscar and Gloria are from Spain. *Are they from* _____ Madrid?

2. Akira is from Japan. _____ Tokyo?

3. Julia is from Brazil. _____ Rio de Janeiro?

4. Florie and her sister are from the Philippines. _____ Manila?

5. Dorothy is from England. _____ London?

6. Mohsen is from Egypt. _____ Cairo?

7. Carlo and his wife are from Italy. _____ Rome?

8. Marie is from Canada. _____ Montreal?

9. Bruce and Susan are from the United States. _____ Los Angeles?

10. Rosa is from Mexico. _____ Mexico City?

11. The Du Lacs are from France. _____ Paris?

12. Anna is from Greece. _____ Athens?

MAKE IT WORK

Fill in the dialogue with a question.

■ Where are you from?

☐ Japan.

■ Oh. _____?

☐ No. I'm from Osaka.

20

HE ISN'T HERE RIGHT NOW.

Negative Statements

Verb *To Be*

He	isn't	here right now.	They	aren't	here right now.
She	isn't	here right now.			

Note: isn't = is not   aren't = are not

he's not/she's not = he/she isn't

they're not = they aren't

PRACTICE

Make negative sentences.

1. Is Loi there? _No. He isn't here right now._

2. Is Louise there? _____

3. Are Louise and Raymond there? _____

4. Is Anna there? _____

5. Are Gloria and Oscar there? _____

6. Is Mohsen there? _____

7. Are Mr. and Mrs. Alba there? _____

8. Are Chang and Lee there? _____

9. Is Julia there? _____

10. Is Rafael there? _____

MAKE IT WORK

Fill in the blanks.

■ Is Gloria Sánchez there?

☐ No. _____

■ Is her husband there?

☐ No. I'm sorry. Her _____

_____ either.

JOHN AND CARMEN AREN'T MARRIED.

Negative and Affirmative Statements
Verb *To Be*

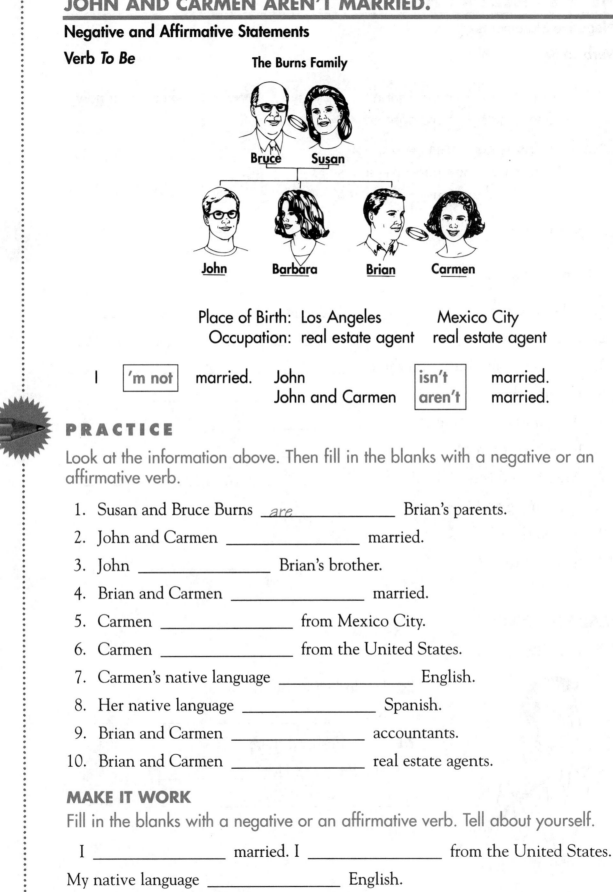

The Burns Family

Bruce   Susan

John   Barbara   Brian   Carmen

Place of Birth: Los Angeles   Mexico City
Occupation: real estate agent   real estate agent

I   **'m not**   married.   John   **isn't**   married.
John and Carmen   **aren't**   married.

PRACTICE

Look at the information above. Then fill in the blanks with a negative or an affirmative verb.

1. Susan and Bruce Burns _are_____ Brian's parents.

2. John and Carmen _____ married.

3. John _____ Brian's brother.

4. Brian and Carmen _____ married.

5. Carmen _____ from Mexico City.

6. Carmen _____ from the United States.

7. Carmen's native language _____ English.

8. Her native language _____ Spanish.

9. Brian and Carmen _____ accountants.

10. Brian and Carmen _____ real estate agents.

MAKE IT WORK

Fill in the blanks with a negative or an affirmative verb. Tell about yourself.

I _____ married. I _____ from the United States.

My native language _____ English.

22

IS LOUISE A HAIRDRESSER? YES, SHE IS.

Negative and Affirmative Short Answers

Verb *To Be*

Are you from France?	Yes, I am.	No, I'm not.
Am I from France?	Yes, you are.	No, you aren't.
Is he from France?	Yes, he is.	No, he isn't.
Is she from France?	Yes, she is.	No, she isn't.
Are you from France?	Yes, we are.	No, we aren't.
Are they from France?	Yes, they are.	No, they aren't.

Note: Affirmative short answers have no contractions.

PRACTICE

Answer the questions with short answers.

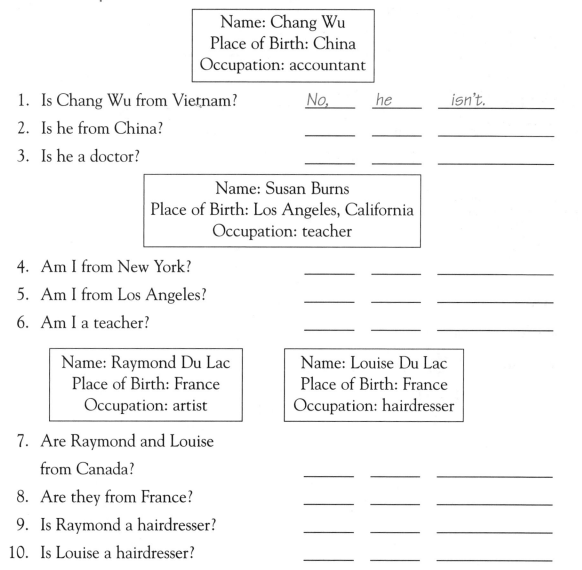

Name: Chang Wu
Place of Birth: China
Occupation: accountant

1. Is Chang Wu from Vietnam?   *No,*   *he*   *isn't.*

2. Is he from China?   _____ _____ _____

3. Is he a doctor?   _____ _____ _____

Name: Susan Burns
Place of Birth: Los Angeles, California
Occupation: teacher

4. Am I from New York?   _____ _____ _____

5. Am I from Los Angeles?   _____ _____ _____

6. Am I a teacher?   _____ _____ _____

Name: Raymond Du Lac
Place of Birth: France
Occupation: artist

Name: Louise Du Lac
Place of Birth: France
Occupation: hairdresser

7. Are Raymond and Louise
   from Canada?   _____ _____ _____

8. Are they from France?   _____ _____ _____

9. Is Raymond a hairdresser?   _____ _____ _____

10. Is Louise a hairdresser?   _____ _____ _____

> Name: Rosa Camino
> Place of Birth: Mexico City, Mexico
> Occupation: nurse

11. Is Rosa Camino from France? _____ _____ _____

12. Is she Spanish? _____ _____ _____

13. Is she from Mexico? _____ _____ _____

14. Is she from Acapulco? _____ _____ _____

15. Is she a doctor? _____ _____ _____

> Name: Oscar Sánchez
> Place of Birth: Seville, Spain
> Occupation: dentist

> Name: Gloria Sánchez
> Place of Birth: Madrid, Spain
> Occupation: interior decorator

16. Are Oscar and Gloria Sánchez
    from Spain? _____ _____ _____

17. Is Oscar from Seville? _____ _____ _____

18. Is Gloria from Seville? _____ _____ _____

19. Are Oscar and Gloria Spanish? _____ _____ _____

20. Are they lawyers? _____ _____ _____

21. Is Gloria a dentist? _____ _____ _____

22. Is Oscar a dentist? _____ _____ _____

MAKE IT WORK

Answer the questions.

Are you from England? _____ _____ _____

Are you an ESL student?

QUEBEC IS A BEAUTIFUL CITY.

Word Order with Statements and Questions

Verb *To Be*

	TO BE	SUBJECT	TO BE	
statement		I	'm	from the United States.
question	Are	you		from Los Angeles?

Note: Each sentence begins with a capital letter and ends with a period (.) or a question mark (?).

PRACTICE

Put the words in the correct order.

1. ■ John Burns/ I'm/.

   I'm John Burns.

2. □ is/ name/ my/ Marie Du Lac/.

   _____

3. ■ are/ the United States/ from/ you/?

   _____

4. □ not/ no,/ I'm/.   am/ I/ Canada/ from/.

   _____

5. ■ you/ are/ Montreal/ from/?

   _____

6. □ I'm/ not/ no,/.   Quebec/ am/ I/ from/.

   _____

7. ■ beautiful/ Quebec/ city/ is/ a/. you/ are/ French/?

   _____

8. □ am/ Canadian/ I/.   French/ language/ is/ my/ native/.

   _____

9. ■ you/ American/ are/?

   _____

10. □ am/ yes,/ I/.   Los Angeles/ from/ I'm/.

    _____

IT'S NINE O'CLOCK.

It with time

Verb *To Be*

It's 9:00.
nine o'clock

9:15
nine fifteen

9:20
nine twenty

9:30
nine thirty

9:45
nine forty five

9:50
nine fifty

Numbers:

1	one	11	eleven	21	twenty-one
2	two	12	twelve	22	twenty-two
3	three	13	thirteen	30	thirty
4	four	14	fourteen	31	thirty-one
5	five	15	fifteen	40	forty
6	six	16	sixteen	50	fifty
7	seven	17	seventeen	60	sixty
8	eight	18	eighteen		
9	nine	19	nineteen		
10	ten	20	twenty		

IT'S NINE O'CLOCK.

PRACTICE

Look at page 26. Then write the time in words.

1. _It's two o'clock._

2. _____

3. _____

4. _____

5. _____

6. _____

7. _____

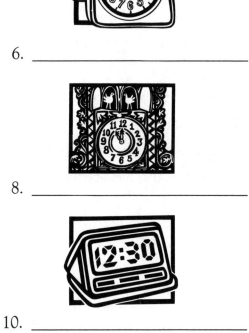

8. _____

9. _____

10. _____

MAKE IT WORK

Answer the question.

What time is it now? _____

27

HE'S NEVER LATE FOR WORK.

Adverbs of Frequency

Verb *To Be*

always	X	X	X	X	X
usually	X	X	X	X	
often	X	X	X		
sometimes	X	X			
rarely	X				
never					

He's early.
He's always early.
He's never early.
Note: Adverbs of frequency usually come after the verb *to be*.

PRACTICE

Add the adverbs to the sentences.

1. Dr. Lau is at his office. (always)   *Dr. Lau is always at his office.*

2. He's late for work. (never)   _____

3. He's early. (sometimes)   _____

4. At his office, he's busy. (usually)   _____
   _____

5. He's tired, too. (often)   _____

6. But he's angry. (rarely)   _____

7. He's nice to his patients. (usually)   _____
   _____

8. His patients are nervous. (sometimes)   _____
   _____

9. But Dr. Lau is nervous. (never)   _____

10. He's friendly to everyone. (always)   _____
    _____

MAKE IT WORK

Tell about yourself. Use an adverb of frequency.

I _____ on time to class.

New Words: patient = a person who visits a doctor

It's 9:00.

He's on time.

He's late.

He's early.

Money and Numbers

How to write checks.

$1.00 One and No/100————————Dollars
$15.00 Fifteen and No/100————————Dollars
$25.99 Twenty-five and 99/100————————Dollars

Note: In U.S. money, $ = dollar, ¢ = cent, and $1.00 = 100 cents.

PRACTICE

Write the following numbers. If necessary, check the appendix for numbers.

1. $17.06   *Seventeen and 06/100* _____ Dollars
2. $15.76   _____ Dollars
3. $39.95   _____ Dollars
4. $19.99   _____ Dollars
5. $45.00   _____ Dollars
6. $50.80   _____ Dollars
7. $92.75   _____ Dollars
8. $63.54   _____ Dollars
9. $88.99   _____ Dollars
10. $74.00   _____ Dollars

MAKE IT WORK

Write $28.07 on this check. Then fill in the date and sign the check.

1173

_____ 19_____

PAY TO THE ORDER OF _Marie Du Lac_ _____ $ _____

D O L L A R S

National Bank
Any City, State

Memo_____   _____

1:220002581:16133830211

TWO HAIRBRUSHES FOR $5.45

Regular Noun Plurals: -s, -es

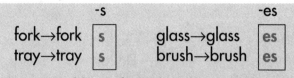

Note: Add *s* to form the plural. Add *es* to form the plural of words ending in *s, sh, ch, x,* or *z.*

PRACTICE

Fill in the blanks with the correct plural form.

1. one spoon for $2.00   twelve _spoons_ for $10.00

2. one fork for $2.00   twelve _____ for $10.00

3. one napkin for $3.50   four _____ for $12.50

4. one dish for $3.59   four _____ for $12.98

5. one pan for $8.99   two _____ for $16.00

6. one glass for $1.25   eight _____ for $8.00

7. one cup for $2.00   two _____ for $3.49

8. one plate for $4.99   eight _____ for $35.99

9.   one hairbrush for $2.89   two _____ for $5.45

10.   one tray for $1.25   two _____ for $1.99

11.   one chair for $18.99   four _____ for $69.99

12.   one couch for $599.00   two _____ for $999.95

13.   one toaster for $25.79   two _____ for $41.99

14.   one jewelry box for $9.00   two _____ for $15.00

15.   one blanket for $29.00   two _____ for $50.00

16.   one clock for $13.47   two _____ for $24.99

17.   one watch for $43.99   two _____ for $71.00

18.   one purse for $29.95   two _____ for $49.95

19.   one dress for $25.00   two _____ for $40.00

20.   one shirt for $20.00   two _____ for $35.00

CHERRIES ARE ONLY $1.99 A POUND.

Regular Noun Plurals: *-s, -es, -ies*

Verb *To Be*

-s	-es	-ies
carrot→carrot `s`	radish→radish `es`	berry→berr `ies`
	potato→potato `es`	
	tomato→tomato `es`	

Note: For words ending in a consonant + *y*, drop the *y* and add *ies*:

berry consonant →berries
y

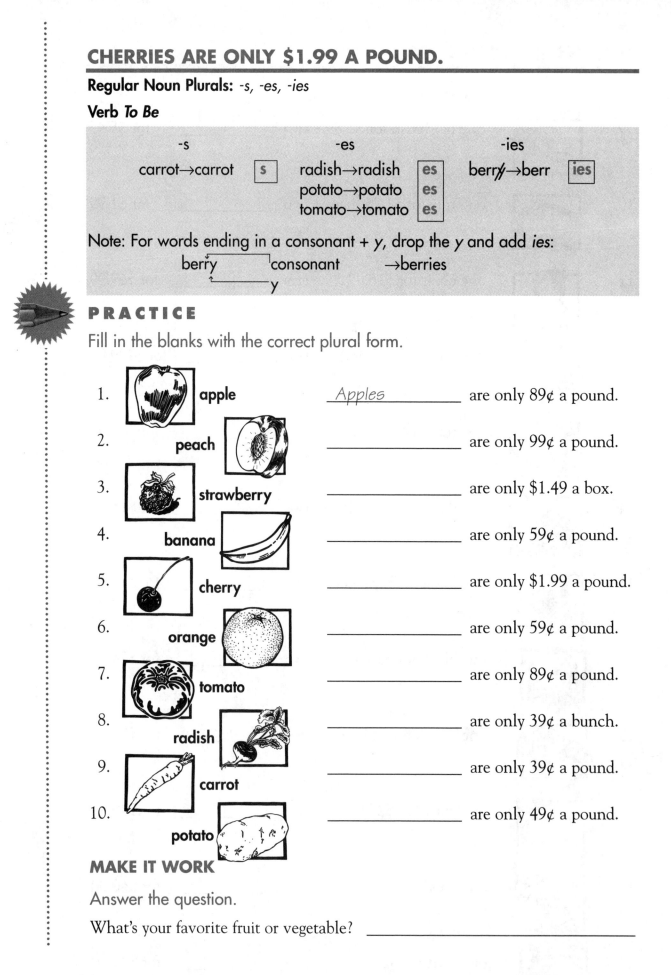

P R A C T I C E

Fill in the blanks with the correct plural form.

1. apple — _Apples_ are only 89¢ a pound.

2. peach — _____ are only 99¢ a pound.

3. strawberry — _____ are only $1.49 a box.

4. banana — _____ are only 59¢ a pound.

5. cherry — _____ are only $1.99 a pound.

6. orange — _____ are only 59¢ a pound.

7. tomato — _____ are only 89¢ a pound.

8. radish — _____ are only 39¢ a bunch.

9. carrot — _____ are only 39¢ a pound.

10. potato — _____ are only 49¢ a pound.

MAKE IT WORK

Answer the question.

What's your favorite fruit or vegetable? _____

32

SHOES FOR MEN

Irregular Noun Plurals

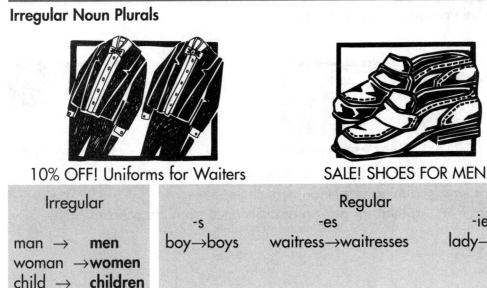

10% OFF! Uniforms for Waiters

SALE! SHOES FOR MEN

Irregular	Regular		
	-s	-es	-ies
man → **men** woman → **women** child → **children**	boy→boys	waitress→waitresses	lady→ladies

PRACTICE

Fill in the blanks with the correct plural form.

1. Half Price! SHOES FOR ___*men*___ (man)

2. Reduced! PURSES FOR _____ (woman)

3. 10% Off! DRESSES FOR _____ (lady)

4. Clearance! T-SHIRTS FOR _____ (boy)

5. 20% Off! HATS FOR _____ (construction worker)

6. Half Price! SHOES FOR _____ (child)

7. 20% Off! BLANKETS FOR _____ (baby)

8. Half Price! UNIFORMS FOR _____ (nurse)

9. SALE! DRESSES FOR _____ (girl)

10. 10% Off! UNIFORMS FOR _____ (waitress)

MAKE IT WORK

Look at the advertisement. Then answer the question.

What's on sale?

_____ for _____

THAT'S MY CAMERA.

Demonstrative Pronouns: *This and That*

Verb *To Be*

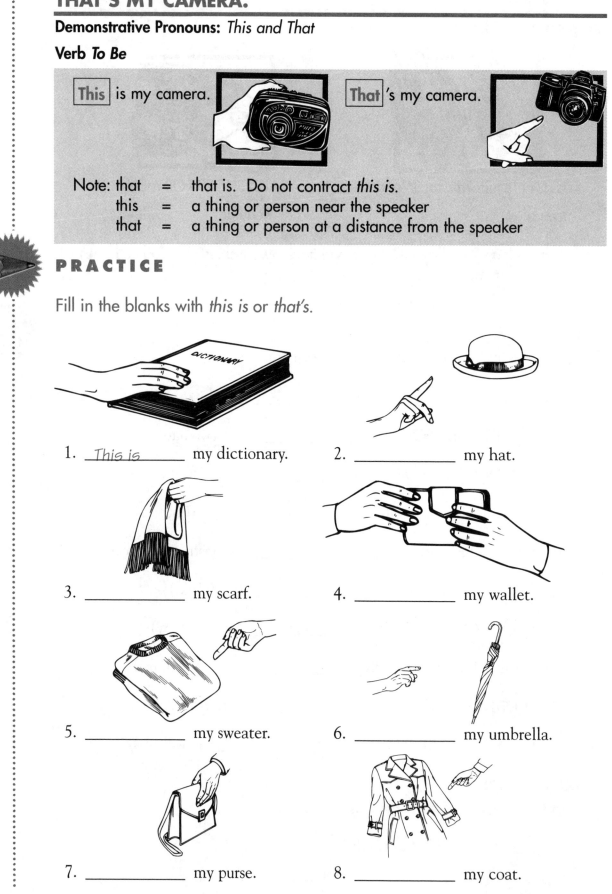

| This | is my camera. |
| That | 's my camera. |

Note: that = that is. Do not contract *this is*.
this = a thing or person near the speaker
that = a thing or person at a distance from the speaker

PRACTICE

Fill in the blanks with *this is* or *that's*.

1. _This is_ my dictionary.

2. _____ my hat.

3. _____ my scarf.

4. _____ my wallet.

5. _____ my sweater.

6. _____ my umbrella.

7. _____ my purse.

8. _____ my coat.

ARE THESE YOUR KEYS?

Demonstrative Pronouns: *These* and *Those*

Verb *To Be*

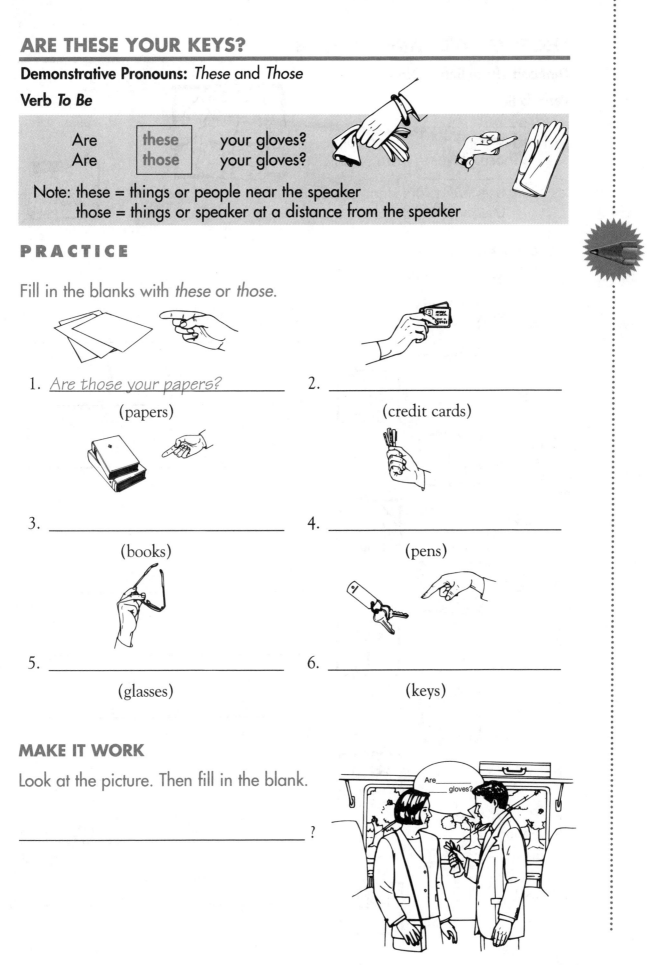

Are | these | your gloves?
Are | those | your gloves?

Note: these = things or people near the speaker
those = things or speaker at a distance from the speaker

PRACTICE

Fill in the blanks with *these* or *those*.

1. *Are those your papers?*
   (papers)

2. _____
   (credit cards)

3. _____
   (books)

4. _____
   (pens)

5. _____
   (glasses)

6. _____
   (keys)

MAKE IT WORK

Look at the picture. Then fill in the blank.

Are_____ _____ gloves?

_____ ?

THOSE GLOVES ARE ON SALE.

That and *Those* Before Nouns

Verb *To Be*

That coat	is on sale.
Those gloves	are on sale.

Note: Use *that* before singular nouns.
Use *those* before plural nouns.

PRACTICE

Make sentences with *that* or *those*.

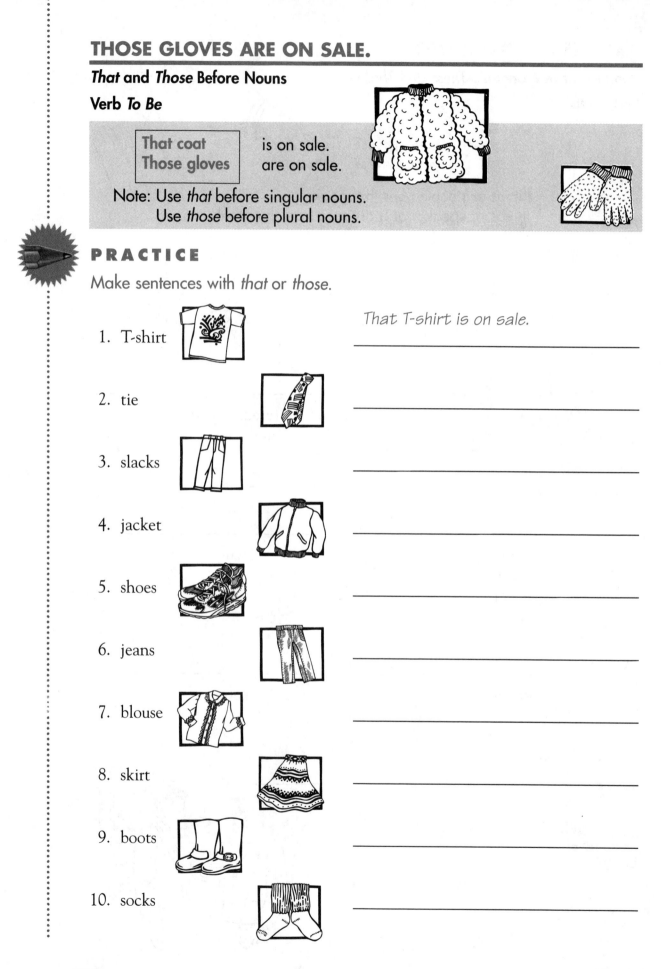

1. T-shirt   *That T-shirt is on sale.*
   _____

2. tie
   _____

3. slacks
   _____

4. jacket
   _____

5. shoes
   _____

6. jeans
   _____

7. blouse
   _____

8. skirt
   _____

9. boots
   _____

10. socks
   _____

THESE DRESSES ARE BEAUTIFUL.

These and *Those* Before Nouns

Verb *To Be*

This dress	is beautiful.
These dresses	are beautiful.
That dress	is ugly.
Those dresses	are ugly.

PRACTICE

Make the sentences plural.

1. This watch is beautiful.   *These watches are beautiful.*
2. That jacket is nice. _____
3. This T-shirt is great. _____
4. This wallet is pretty. _____
5. That purse is nice. _____
6. That sweater is beautiful. _____
7. That tie is pretty. _____
8. This coat is ugly. _____
9. That shirt is nice. _____
10. That blouse is pretty. _____
11. This dress is beautiful. _____
12. This hat is great. _____

MAKE IT WORK

Comment about a friend's gloves.

_____

Comment about a friend's shoes.

_____

■ That sweater is nice.

☐ Thank you.

HOW MUCH ARE THEY?

Questions with *How Much*
Verb *To Be*

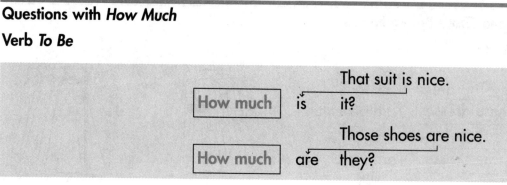

			That suit is nice.
How much	is	it?	
			Those shoes are nice.
How much	are	they?	

PRACTICE

Make questions with *how much.*

1. These T-shirts are great.   _How much are they?_
2. This tie is beautiful.   _____
3. That jacket is pretty.   _____
4. Those slacks are nice.   _____
5. These shoes are beautiful.   _____
6. This blouse is pretty.   _____
7. Those gloves are nice.   _____
8. These sunglasses are great.   _____
9. That sweater is beautiful.   _____
10. This dress is nice.   _____
11. Those boots are great.   _____
12. That umbrella is pretty.   _____

MAKE IT WORK

Make questions with *how much.*

   _____

   _____

   _____

38

WHO IS HIS TEACHER?

Questions with *Who, What, Where*

Verb *To Be*

What class	is he in?	French
What time	is his class?	4:00 P.M.
Who	is his teacher?	Mrs. Breyer
Where	is his class?	North Hall

PRACTICE

Fill in the blanks *what class, what time, who,* or *where.*

1. _____What class_____ is he in?   ESL 1
2. _____ is his teacher?   Mrs. Breyer
3. _____ is his class?   523 Main Building
4. _____ is his class?   6:00 P.M.
5. _____ is her teacher?   Mrs. Burns
6. _____ is her class?   11:00 A.M.
7. _____ is her class?   South Hall
8. _____ is she in?   ESL 3
9. _____ is she in?   Spanish 2
10. _____ is her teacher?   Miss Garcia
11. _____ is his class?   8:45 A.M.
12. _____ is his teacher   Mr. Burns
13. _____ is he in?   Math
14. _____ is his class?   Room 311

Note: A.M. = morning
P.M. = evening or afternoon

morning

afternoon

evening

WHERE IS HIS CLASS?

Questions with *Who, What, Where*

Verb *To Be*

Where	is his class?
	It's in 43 South Hall.

PRACTICE

Look at the registration forms. Then make questions with *what class*, *where*, *what time*, and *who*.

Name: Akira Ito
Class: ESL 1
Room: 43 South Hall
Time: 6:00 P.M.
Teacher: Mrs. Burns

1. *What class is he in?*
2. _____
3. _____
4. _____

Name: Loi Van Ha
Class: Auto Mechanics
Teacher: Mr. Smith
Time: 7:30 P.M.
Room: 23 Dodge Hall

5. _____
6. _____
7. _____
8. _____

Name: Anna Thanos
Class: Accounting 1A
Instructor: Mr. Brown
Room: 100 Main Building
Time: 11:00 A.M.

9. _____
10. _____
11. _____
12. _____

MAKE IT WORK

Fill in the registration form with information about yourself.

REGISTRATION FORM
Name:
Class:
Room:
Time:
Teacher:

40

I'M IN MATH 1A THIS SEMESTER.

Review: Long and Short Answers
Verb *To Be*

Are you a student?	Yes, I am.
What class are you in?	I'm in Math 1A this semester.
Is it interesting or boring?	It's boring.

PRACTICE

Answer the questions.

1. What's your name? _____

2. Where are you from? _____

3. What's your native language? _____

4. What's your occupation? _____

5. What's your telephone number? _____

6. What class (or classes) are
   you in this semester? _____

7. Is this your first English class? _____

8. Is this class easy or difficult
   for you? _____

9. Is this class interesting or boring? _____

10. Who's your teacher? _____

11. Is he (or she) a good teacher? _____

12. Where is your teacher from? _____

MAKE IT WORK

Fill in the form with information about yourself.

REGISTRATION FORM:

Name: _____

Address: _____

Home Telephone Number: _____ Place of Birth: _____

Occupation: _____

Work Address: _____ Work Telephone Number: _____

MY HUSBAND AND I ARE TEACHERS.

Review: Verb *To Be*

My name	**is**	Susan Burns.
I	**'m**	married.
My husband and I	**are**	teachers.

PRACTICE

Fill in the blanks with *am*, *are*, or *is*. Use contractions whenever possible.

My name _is_ (1) Susan Burns. I _____ (2) married. My

husband and I _____ (3) from Los Angeles. We _____ (4) teachers.

My husband _____ (5) a math teacher, and I _____ (6) an ESL teacher.

Our son John _____ (7) 21, and our daughter Barbara _____ (8) 19.

They _____ (9) students at Fullerton College. Fullerton _____ (10) a city

in California. Our son Brian _____ (11) married. He _____ (12) a real estate

agent. My parents _____ (13) still alive. My mother _____ (14) 78, and my

father _____ (15) 85. They _____ (16) retired now. My sister, Diane,

_____ (17) divorced. She _____ (18) a cashier in a drugstore in Los Angeles.

MAKE IT WORK

Tell about yourself and your family.

_____

_____

_____

_____

New Words: retired = no longer working at an occupation
alive = living
divorced = no longer married

42

THE KNIFE IS ON THE COUNTER.

Prepositions of Place: *In and On*

Verb *To Be*

The pan is | on | the stove.   The pan is | in | the oven.

| in | the drawer | in | the cupboard | in | the refrigerator

| on | the counter | on | the shelf | on | the table

PRACTICE

Fill in the blanks with *in* or *on*.

1. The glasses are __in__ the cupboard.

2. The toaster is __on__ the counter.

3. The plates are __in__ the cupboard.

4. The napkins are __on__ the shelf.

5. The cups are __in__ the cupboard.

6. The knife is __on__ the counter.

7. The spoons are __in__ the drawer.

8. The tomatoes are __in__ the refrigerator.

9. The sugar bowl is __on__ the table.

10. The pan is __in__ the oven.

11. The forks are __in__ the drawer.

12. The strawberries are __in__ the refrigerator.

13. The pan is __on__ the stove.

14. The stove is __in__ the kitchen.

MAKE IT WORK

Look at the picture. Then fill in the blank with *in* or *on*.

The telephone book is _____ the cabinet.

43

Affirmative Statements

There Is and *There Are*

windows

electrical outlet

fireplace

living room

refrigerator

counter

sinks

kitchen

tiles

shower

toilet

bathtub

sink

bathroom

window

closet

bedroom

THERE'S A FIREPLACE IN THE LIVING ROOM.

| There's | a kitchen in the apartment. |
| There are | four rooms in the apartment. |

Note: There's → there is *Do not contract there are.*
Use *there is* with singular forms.
Use *there are* with plural forms.

PRACTICE

Fill in the blanks with *there's* or *there are*.

1. *There are*_____ four rooms in the apartment.

2. _____ a living room in the apartment.

3. _____ a fireplace in the living room.

4. _____ two large windows in the living room.

5. _____ a kitchen in the apartment.

6. _____ a refrigerator in the kitchen.

7. _____ a stove in the kitchen.

8. _____ two sinks in the kitchen.

9. _____ one bedroom in the apartment.

10. _____ a bathroom in the apartment.

11. _____ tiles in the bathroom.

12. _____ a shower in the bathroom.

13. _____ a bathtub in the bathroom.

14. _____ an electrical outlet in the living room.

MAKE IT WORK

Tell about your apartment, room, or house.

_____

_____

_____

THERE'S A REFRIGERATOR IN THE KITCHEN.

Articles *A* and *The*

There Is* and *There Are

There's │ a │ kitchen in the apartment.   There's a refrigerator in │ the │ kitchen.

Note: Use *a* when mentioning something singular for the first time.
Use *the* when something has been mentioned before.

PRACTICE

Fill in the blanks with *a* or *the*.

1. There's __*a*__ living room in the apartment.

2. There's a fireplace in _____ living room.

3. There's a kitchen in _____ apartment.

4. There's _____ refrigerator in the kitchen.

5. There's an electrical outlet in _____ kitchen.

6. There's _____ dishwasher in the kitchen.

7. There's a bedroom in _____ apartment.

8. There's _____ closet in the bedroom.

9. There's a large window in _____ bedroom.

10. There's _____ bathroom in the apartment.

11. There's a bathtub in _____ bathroom.

12. There's _____ shower in the bathroom, too.

13. There's _____ dining room in the apartment.

14. There's _____ window in the dining room.

MAKE IT WORK

Look at the dialogue. Then fill in the blanks.

■ Is there a closet in the bedroom?

☐ Yes. The closet is right over there.

■ _____ dishwasher

_____ ?

☐ Yes. _____ right

over there.

46

IS THERE A DISHWASHER IN THE KITCHEN?

Yes-No Questions

There Is and ***There Are***

There are four rooms in the apartment.

Are there four rooms in the apartment?

There's a washing machine in the apartment.

Is there a washing machine in the apartment?

PRACTICE

Make questions with *is there* and *are there*.

Kitchen

1. (refrigerator)   *Is there a refrigerator in the kitchen?*

2. (dishwasher)   _____

3. (counters)   _____

4. (electrical outlets)   _____

5. (window)   _____

6. (washing machine)   _____

7. (cabinets)   _____

Bathroom

8. (shower)   _____

9. (tiles)   _____

10. (bathtub)   _____

Living Room

11. (windows)   _____

12. (fireplace)   _____

MAKE IT WORK

Ask questions about the apartment for rent.

FOR RENT
Large four-room apartment. Kitchen, bath, bedrooms, living room. $800.00 a month.

Is there a fireplace in the living room?

_____

_____

_____

IS THERE A FIRE DETECTOR IN THE APARTMENT?

Word Order with Yes-No Questions

There Is and *There Are*

to be	there	noun	place
Is	there	a superintendent	in the building?

PRACTICE

Put the words in the correct order.

TEN IMPORTANT QUESTIONS TO ASK BEFORE YOU RENT AN APARTMENT

1. there/ in/ a/ the/ building/ is/ superintendent/?

   Is there a superintendent in the building?

2. door/ lock/ the/ on/ there/ is/ a/?

   _____

3. the/ lights/ there/ are/ hallways/ in/?

   _____

4. building/ in/ a/ washing machine/ is/ the/ there/?

   _____

5. is/ stove/ in/ there/ kitchen/ the/ a/?

   _____

6. there/ are/ apartment/ closets/ the/ in/?

   _____

7. in/ fire detector/ there/ is/ the/ apartment/ a/?

   _____

8. apartment/ the/ there/ electrical outlets/ in/ are/?

   _____

9. windows/ are/ the/ in/ there/ apartment/?

   _____

10. is/ in/ bathroom/ a/ shower/ there/ the/?

   _____

New Words:

| superintendent | fire detector | lock | hallway |

IS THERE A WINDOW IN THE KITCHEN? YES, THERE IS.

Negative and Affirmative Short Answers

There Is and *There Are*

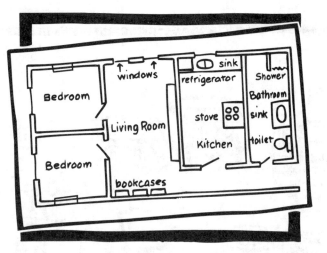

Questions	Answers
Is there a window in the kitchen?	Yes, there is.
Is there a window in the bathroom?	No, there isn't.
Are there bookcases in the living room?	Yes, there are.
Are there bookcases in the bedroom?	No, there aren't.

PRACTICE

Look at the picture. Then answer the questions with short answers.

1. Are there five rooms in the apartment? _Yes, there are._
2. Is there a kitchen in the apartment? _____
3. Are there three bedrooms in the apartment? _____
4. Is there a living room in the apartment? _____
5. Is there a dining room in the apartment? _____
6. Are there windows in the living room? _____
7. Are there bookcases in the living room? _____
8. Is there a washing machine in the kitchen? _____
9. Are there closets in the bedrooms? _____
10. Is there a shower in the bathroom? _____
11. Are there two sinks in the bathroom? _____
12. Is there a bathtub in the bathroom? _____

MAKE IT WORK

Answer the question.

Is there a fire detector in your house or apartment? _____

THERE'S SOME MEAT ON THE PLATES.

Some with Countable and Uncountable Nouns

There Is and *There Are*

THERE'S SOME MEAT ON THE PLATES.

There are	some	large plates on the table.
There's	some	meat on the plates.

Note: Use *some* for unspecified quantities. Use *some* with plural countable nouns. Uncountable nouns take singular verb forms:

There is some   water   meat   salt   coffee
                soda   ice   bread   rice

PRACTICE

Fill in the blanks with the correct verb form and *some*. Use contractions whenever possible.

1. _There are some_ _____ plates on the table.

2. _____ glasses on the table.

3. _____ napkins on the table.

4. _____ bottles on the table.

5. _____ soda in the bottles.

6. _____ forks on the table.

7. _____ salt on the table.

8. _____ pitchers on the table.

9. _____ ice in the pitchers.

10. _____ water in the pitchers.

11. _____ large plates on the table.

12. _____ meat on the plates.

13. _____ bowls on the table.

14. _____ rice in the bowls.

15. _____ large bowls on the table.

16. _____ vegetables in the bowls.

17. _____ baskets on the table.

18. _____ bread in the baskets.

19. _____ cups on the table.

20. _____ coffee on the table.

THERE'S SOME SALT ON THE TABLE.

A with Countable Nouns and *Some* with Uncountable Nouns

There Is

There's a glass on the table. There's some water in the glass.

Note: Use *some* before these uncountable nouns: water   cream   coffee
sugar   salt   pepper

PRACTICE

Fill in the blanks with *a* or *some*.

1. There's ___*a*___ glass on the table.

2. There's ___*some*___ water in the glass.

3. There's _____ plate on the table.

4. There's _____ fork on the table.

5. There's _____ knife on the table.

6. There's _____ pitcher on the table.

7. There's _____ cream in the pitcher.

8. There's _____ salt on the table.

9. There's _____ pepper on the table.

10. There's _____ bowl on the table.

11. There's _____ sugar in the bowl.

12. There's _____ spoon on the table.

13. There's _____ cup on the table.

14. There's _____ coffee in the cup.

MAKE IT WORK

Name one thing on the counter in your kitchen.

THERE ISN'T ANY WATER IN THE PITCHERS.

Any with Negative Statements

There Is and *There Are*

There are some pitchers on the table.

There $\boxed{\text{isn't any}}$ water in the pitchers.

Note: Use *any* in negative statements with plural countable nouns or with uncountable nouns.

PRACTICE

Look at the picture above. Then make negative sentences.

1. plates   *There aren't any plates on the table.*

2. rice   *There isn't any rice on the table.*

3. glasses   _____

4. napkins   _____

5. meat   _____

6. water   _____

7. vegetables   _____

8. bread   _____

9. soda   _____

10. pepper   _____

11. salt   _____

12. cups   _____

13. coffee   _____

14. spoons   _____

Countable and Uncountable Nouns

PRACTICE

Look at the picture above. Then write the name of each food in the appropriate category.

singular countable nouns	plural countable nouns	uncountable nouns
a lemon	_eggs_	_milk_
_____	_____	_____
_____	_____	_____
	_____	_____
		_____
		_____

MAKE IT WORK

Make a list of some things you need from the supermarket.

_____

_____

_____

_____

_____

_____

Some and *Any* with Affirmative and Negative Statements

There Is and *There Are*

There's	a lemon	in the refrigerator.
There are	some eggs	in the refrigerator.
There isn't	any meat	in the refrigerator.
There aren't	any apples	in the refrigerator.

P R A C T I C E

Look at the picture on page 54. Then make negative and affirmative sentences.

1. lettuce   *There's some lettuce in the refrigerator.*

2. meat   *There isn't any meat in the refrigerator.*

3. a lemon   _____

4. carrots   _____

5. milk   _____

6. cream   _____

7. a tomato   _____

8. strawberries   _____

9. soda   _____

10. apples   _____

11. mayonnaise   _____

12. a cucumber   _____

13. eggs   _____

14. coffee   _____

15. oranges   _____

16. orange juice   _____

MAKE IT WORK

Name one thing in your refrigerator.

_____

IS THERE ANY SODA?

Any with Yes-No Questions

There Is and There Are

> Is there [any] soda?
> Are there [any] eggs?
>
> Note: You can use *any* with countable and uncountable nouns in questions.

PRACTICE

Make questions with *any*.

1. *Is there any ice cream?*   No. We're out of ice cream.

2. _____ No. We're out of soda.

3. _____ No. We're out of tomatoes.

4. _____ No. We're out of rice.

5. _____ No. We're out of milk.

6. _____ No. We're out of eggs.

7. _____ No. We're out of napkins.

8. _____ No. We're out of bread.

9. _____ No. We're out of coffee.

10. _____ No. We're out of potatoes.

11. _____ No. We're out of margarine.

12. _____ No. We're out of carrots.

MAKE IT WORK

Fill in the blanks with questions.

■ I'm hungry. _____?

☐ No. We're out of ice cream.

■ _____?

☐ Sorry. We're out of strawberries.

THERE'S A BOOKCASE IN THE CLASSROOM.

Review: *There Is, There Are*, Prepositions, Articles, Word Order

there	*to be*		noun	place
There	's	a	bookcase	in the classroom.
There	are	some	books	in the bookcase.
There	's	a	clock	on the wall.

PRACTICE

Look at the picture. Then make some sentences about the classroom.

1. *There are ten chairs in the classroom.*
2. _____
3. _____
4. _____
5. _____
6. _____
7. _____
8. _____
9. _____
10. _____

MAKE IT WORK

Tell about your classroom.

_____
_____
_____
_____
_____

A LITTLE BOY IS EATING AN ICE CREAM CONE.

Affirmative Statements

Present Continuous

A LITTLE BOY IS EATING AN ICE CREAM CONE.

A man is reading. Two men are reading.

cook + ing = cooking
sleep + ing = sleeping
play + ing = playing
write + ing = writing

Note: present continuous: *am / is / are* + verb + *ing*
To form the present continuous of a verb that ends in *y*, add *ing*.
If a verb ends in *e*, drop the *e* and add *ing*.
Use the present continuous for actions that are happening now.

PRACTICE

Fill in the blanks with the correct form of the verb.

1. (cook)   A man and a woman _are cooking_____.

2. (eat)   A little boy _____ an ice cream cone.

3. (read)   A man _____.

4. (play)   Two teenage boys _____ cards.

5. (sleep)   A baby _____.

6. (talk)   A young man and woman _____.

7. (take)   A tall man _____ a walk.

8. (fly)   A boy and his father _____ a kite.

9. (play)   A young man _____ a guitar.

10. (look)   A woman _____ at the sky.

11. (listen) Two teenage girls _____ to the radio.

12. (hold)   A little girl _____ a flower.

13. (fish)   A man _____.

MAKE IT WORK

Answer the question.

What are you doing now? I'm _____

SHE'S WEARING A SUIT.

Affirmative Statements

Present Continuous

I	'm wearing	a suit.
You	're wearing	a suit.
He	's wearing	a suit.
She	's wearing	a suit.
We	're wearing	suits.
They	're wearing	suits.

long forms: am   are   is
contractions: 'm   're   's

PRACTICE

Fill in the blanks with the correct form of the verb. Use contractions whenever possible.

I'm Connie Rivera here at the Garden Hotel in London. Today

we _'re watching_____ a fashion show. Here are two beautiful suits for any office.
       (1. watch)

Joan _____ a fabulous black suit. And here's Kevin in a gray suit.
       (2. wear)

He _____ a white shirt and a striped tie. Their suits are from the
       (3. wear)

Fifth Avenue Collection. They _____ briefcases by Exclusive Imports.
                               (4. carry)

If you _____ for an evening dress, here's Patricia in a long dress.
       (5. look)

She _____ black, the perfect color for evening. She _____
       (6. wear)   (7. carry)

a black jacket. And here's Joan. She _____ a short white skirt
                                      (8. wear)

and a white blouse. They _____ evening bags by Rags to Riches.
                          (9. hold)

They _____ earrings by Franco di Amato. They're very elegant,
       (10. wear)

aren't they?

MAKE IT WORK

Answer the question.

What are you wearing today? _____

New Words: bag = purse   earrings

60

HE'S SITTING IN A CHAIR.

Spelling

Present Continuous

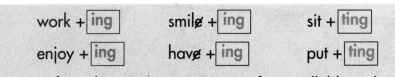

work + ing   smil$\cancel{e}$ + ing   sit + ting

enjoy + ing   hav$\cancel{e}$ + ing   put + ting

Note: To form the present continuous of one-syllable verbs ending in consonant + vowel + consonant, double the consonant before adding *ing*.

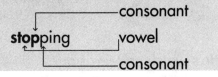

stopping

consonant
vowel
consonant

PRACTICE

Add *ing* to the verbs below. Be sure to double the consonant or cross out the e (é) if necessary.

1. He's sit_ting_ in a chair.

2. He's smile_____.

3. He's drink_____ an orange soda.

4. He's have_____ a snack.

5. He's relax_____.

6. He's watch_____ television.

7. He's enjoy_____ the television program.

8. She's work_____.

9. She's stand_____ in the kitchen.

10. She's put_____ the dishes on the table.

11. She's set_____ the table.

12. She's isn't smile_____.

13. She's frown_____.

14. She's get_____ dinner ready.

MAKE IT WORK

Tell about each picture. What is she doing?

_____   _____

THEY AREN'T WATCHING TELEVISION.

Negative Statements

Present Continuous

		He's watching television.
She	isn't	watching television.
They	aren't	watching television.

contractions: isn't = is not   aren't = are not

PRACTICE

Look at the pictures above. Then make negative sentences.

The man is sitting down.

1. The woman _isn't sitting down._

2. The boys _____

He's drinking soda.

3. She _____

4. They _____

He's relaxing.

5. She _____

6. They _____

He's watching television.

7. She _____

8. They _____

He's smiling.

9. She _____

10. They _____

He's enjoying the
television program.

11. She _____

_____

12. They _____

_____

He's having a good time.

13. She _____

14. They _____

SHE ISN'T WEARING A HAT.

Negative and Affirmative Statements

Present Continuous

| She | 's | wearing a scarf. |
| She | isn't | wearing a hat. |

PRACTICE

Look at the picture above. Then make negative and affirmative sentences.

1. slacks   *She isn't wearing slacks.*
2. a skirt   _____
3. a jacket   _____
4. sneakers   _____
5. a blouse   _____
6. boots   _____
7. a raincoat   _____
8. a suit   _____
9. a briefcase _____
10. an umbrella _____
11. a hat   _____
12. a scarf   _____

MAKE IT WORK

Tell what's unusual about the picture.

_____

_____

_____

IS SHE SLEEPING?

Yes-No Questions

Present Continuous

They're eating.

Are they eating?

PRACTICE

Make questions.

Gloria is in the kitchen.

1. (cook) *Is she cooking?* _____

2. (set the table) _____

   _____

3. (eat) _____

4. (get dinner ready) _____

   _____

5. (wash the dishes) _____

   _____

Pedro and Alfonso are in the den.

6. (watch television) _____

   _____

7. (play cards) _____

8. (listen to the radio) _____

   _____

Maria is in the bedroom.

9. (relax) _____

10. (sleep) _____

11. (read) _____

12. (talk on the telephone) _____

    _____

Oscar and Rafael are in the living room.

13. (talk) _____

14. (drink soda) _____

15. (have a good time) _____

    _____

IS THE GIRL WINNING THE GAME? YES, SHE IS.

Negative and Affirmative Short Answers

Present Continuous

Is the girl standing up?
Is the girl sitting down?
Are the man and the girl standing up?
Are the man and the girl sitting down?

Yes, she is.
No, she isn't.
No, they aren't.
Yes, they are.

PRACTICE

Answer the questions with short answers.

1. Are the man and the girl standing up? _No, they aren't._____

2. Are they sitting down? _____

3. Are they talking? _____

4. Are they playing a game? _____

5. Are they playing cards? _____

6. Are they playing chess? _____

7. Is the man smiling? _____

8. Is the girl smiling? _____

9. Is the man enjoying the game? _____

10. Is the girl enjoying the game? _____

11. Is the man winning the game? _____

12. Is the girl winning the game? _____

MAKE IT WORK

Answer the questions.

Are you sitting down? _____

Are you talking? _____

WHAT'S HE DOING?

Questions with *What*

Present Continuous

	What's he doing?	He's reading.
	What's he reading?	A newspaper.

contraction: what's = what is
Do not contract *what are*.

PRACTICE

Look at the pictures. Then make questions with *what*. Answer your questions.

1. *What's he doing?*
   He's reading.

2. _____
   _____

3. _____
   _____

4. _____
   _____

5. _____
   _____

6. _____
   _____

7. _____
   _____

8. _____
   _____

MAKE IT WORK

Answer the questions.

What are you doing now? _____

What are you writing? _____

IT'S RAINING IN LONDON.

It with Weather

Present Continuous

| It | 's sunny in Cairo. |
| It | 's snowing in Montreal. |

☀ sunny 🌬 windy ❄ snowy
☁ cloudy 🌧 rainy

PRACTICE

Look at the weather report. Then make affirmative sentences about the weather in each city. Use contractions.

Today's Weather

Cairo	sunny
Montreal	snowing
Madrid	windy
Los Angeles	cloudy
London	raining
Athens	sunny
Tokyo	cloudy
New York	snowing
Paris	raining
Mexico City	sunny

1. _It's sunny in Cairo._
2. _____
3. _____
4. _____
5. _____
6. _____
7. _____
8. _____
9. _____
10. _____

MAKE IT WORK

Answer the question.

What's the weather like in your city right now?

_____

IN ATHENS, PEOPLE ARE PROBABLY WORKING.

Review: Present Continuous

In Mexico City, people	are	probably	eating	breakfast.

Times Around the World			
Los Angeles	5:00 A.M.	Athens	3:00 P.M.
Mexico City	7:00 A.M.	Bombay	6:30 P.M.
Bogotá	8:00 A.M.	Manila	9:00 P.M.
Rio de Janeiro	10:00 A.M.	Tokyo	10:00 P.M.
London	1:00 P.M.	Wellington, New Zealand	1:00 A.M.

PRACTICE

Look at the times around the world. Then tell what people are probably doing in each city.

1. _In Los Angeles, people are probably sleeping._
2. _____
3. _____
4. _____
5. _____
6. _____
7. _____
8. _____
9. _____
10. _____

MAKE IT WORK

Answer the questions.

What time is it in your country? _____

What are people probably doing now? _____

New Words: breakfast = meal in the morning
              lunch = meal in the middle of the day
              dinner = main meal of the day, usually in the evening in the United States

HE'S GOING TO PLAY TENNIS.

Affirmative Statements

Future with *Going To*

I	'm		
He	's	going to play	tennis.
She	's		
They	're		

Note: future with *going to*: *to be* + *going to* + verb
      Use the future with *going to* for actions that are going to happen in a few minutes, tomorrow, next week, or next month.

PRACTICE

Make sentences with *going to*.

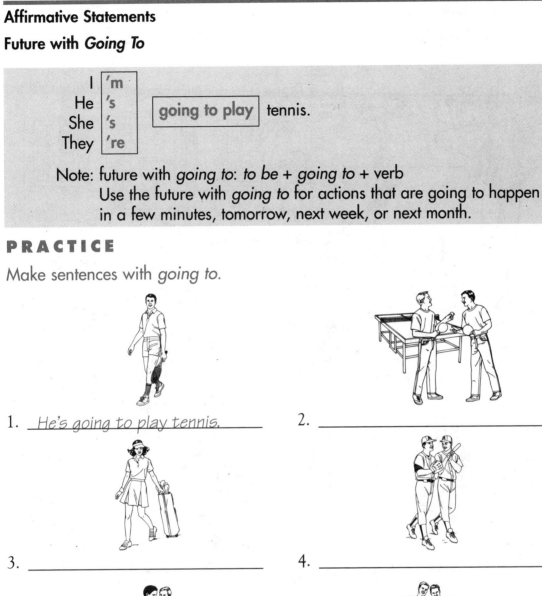

1. <u>He's going to play tennis.</u>   2. _____

3. _____   4. _____

5. _____   6. _____

MAKE IT WORK

Answer the question.

What are you going to do in a few minutes?

_____

69

SUSAN IS GOING TO WORK IN THE YARD.

Affirmative Statements

Future with *Going To*

Barbara

Diane

Carmen

Bruce

Susan

Linda

Brian

Andy

Dorothy

Leonard

Marie

John

70

SUSAN IS GOING TO WORK IN THE YARD.

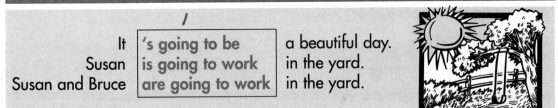

It	's going to be	a beautiful day.
Susan	is going to work	in the yard.
Susan and Bruce	are going to work	in the yard.

PRACTICE

Look at the picture on page 70. Then make sentences using the future with *going to*.

1. (work in the yard)   Susan and Bruce <u>*are working in the yard.*</u>

2. (water the flowers)   Susan _____

3. (mow the lawn)   Bruce _____

4. (wash the car)   Leonard and Dorothy _____

   _____

5. (play tennis)   John and Marie _____

   _____

6. (ride her bicycle)   Linda _____

   _____

7. (swim)   Barbara _____

8. (play baseball)   Brian and Andy _____

   _____

9. (play golf)   Carmen _____

10. (sit in the sun)   Diane _____

   _____

MAKE IT WORK

Answer the questions.

What's the weather going to be like this weekend?

_____

What are you going to do?

_____

IS SHE GOING TO PLAY TENNIS? YES, SHE IS.

Negative and Affirmative Short Answers

Future with *Going To*

Is she going to play cards?
Is she going to play tennis?
Are they going to play cards?
Are they going to play tennis?

| No, she isn't. |
| Yes, she is. |
| No, they aren't. |
| Yes, they are. |

PRACTICE

Look at the pictures. Then answer the questions with short answers.

1. Is she going to wash the car?   _No, she isn't._

2. Is she going to water flowers?   _____

3. Is she going to mow the lawn?   _____

4. Are they going to play football? _____

5. Are they going to play cards?   _____

6. Are they going to play baseball? _____

7. Is she going to play ping-pong?   _____

8. Is she going to play golf?   _____

9. Is she going to play tennis?   _____

10. Are they going to wash the
    windows?   _____

11. Are they going to wash their
    bicycles?   _____

12. Are they going to wash the car? _____

72

LEONARD AND DOROTHY AREN'T GOING TO WASH THE CAR.

Negative Statements

Future with *Going To*

It	**'s**	going to rain.
Dorothy	**isn't**	going to wash the car.
Dorothy and Leonard	**aren't**	going to wash the car.

PRACTICE

Make negative sentences with *going to*.

1. (work in the yard)   Susan and Bruce   *aren't going to work in the yard.*

2. (water the flowers)   Susan _____

_____

3. (mow the lawn)   Bruce _____

_____

4. (wash the car)   Dorothy and Leonard _____

_____

5. (play tennis)   John and Marie _____

_____

6. (ride her bicycle)   Linda _____

_____

7. (swim)   Barbara _____

8. (play baseball)   Brian and Andy _____

_____

9. (play golf)   Carmen _____

10. (sit in the sun)   Diane _____

_____

MAKE IT WORK

Name one thing you aren't going to do this weekend.

_____

THEY AREN'T GOING TO RUN TOMORROW.

Negative Statements
Future with *Going To*

I	'm not	going to run tomorrow.
He	isn't	
She	isn't	
They	aren't	

PRACTICE

Look at the pictures above. Then make negative sentences.

Marie is going to run tomorrow.

1. He _isn't going to run tomorrow._
2. They _____

She's going to exercise tomorrow.

3. He _____
4. They _____

She's going to play soccer tomorrow.

5. He _____
6. They _____

She's going to dance tomorrow.

7. He _____
8. They _____

She's going to take a walk tomorrow.

9. He _____
10. They _____

She's going to work tomorrow.

11. He _____
12. They _____

MAKE IT WORK

Name one thing you aren't going to do tomorrow.

_____

New Word: exercise

WHO IS SHE GOING TO PLAY GOLF WITH?

Questions with *Who, When, What Time*

Future with *Going To*

When Who What time	is Marie going to play golf? is she going to play golf with? is she going to play golf?	MAY 2 golf — Carmen 4:00

Note: informal English: Who . . . with?
       formal English: With whom . . . ?

PRACTICE

Make questions about Marie. Use *who*, *when*, and *what time*.

MAY 2

ping-pong — Arika
2:00

1. _When is she going to play ping-pong?_

2. _____

3. _____

MAY 8

the movies —Anna
6:00 P.M.

4. _____
   _____

5. _____
   _____

6. _____
   _____

MAY 10

dinner — 5:30
Oscar and Gloria

7. _____

8. _____

9. _____

MAY 14

Susan's party — 8:00
John

10. _____
    _____

11. _____
    _____

12. _____
    _____

THEY'RE GOING TO TAKE A LOT OF PICTURES.

Review: Future with *Going To*

She's going to be	in New York.
They're going to be	in New York.

PRACTICE

Read the sentences about Susan. Then rewrite them. Tell about Susan and her husband, Bruce. Change *Susan* to *Susan and Bruce*, and *she* to *they*.

Susan is going to visit New York next month. She's going to be in New York one week so she isn't going to have time to see everything. She's going to take a bus tour of the city. Then she's going to visit the World Trade Center. She's also going to see the Statue of Liberty, but she isn't going to climb the stairs to the top. She's going to eat at some famous restaurants, and she's going to shop on Fifth Avenue. She's going to take her camera. She's going to take a lot of pictures.

Susan and Bruce are going to visit New York next month. They're going to be in New York one week,

_____

_____

_____

_____

_____

_____

_____

_____

_____

_____

New Words: stairs   climb   bus tour

SHE'S GOING TO PLAY TENNIS. SHE'S PLAYING TENNIS.

Contrast: Future with *Going To* vs. Present Continuous

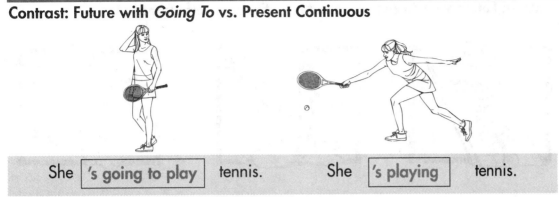

| She | 's going to play | tennis. | She | 's playing | tennis. |

PRACTICE

Look at the pictures. Then fill in the blanks with the correct tense. Use contractions.

1. (wear)   She*'s wearing* sunglasses.

2. (hold)   She_____a tennis racket.

3. (play)   She_____tennis.

4. (take)   He_____a walk.

5. (listen) He_____to the radio.

6. (rain)   It's_____

7. (swim)   They_____

8. (wear)   They_____bathing suits.

9. (hold)   She_____a camera.

10. (take) She_____some pictures.

11. (carry) They_____towels.

12. (stand) They_____near the pool.

PRACTICE

Tell about yourself.

I _____ now.

_____ in a few minutes.

IT'S GOING TO RAIN TOMORROW. IT'S RAINING NOW.

Contrast: Future with *Going To*, Present Continuous, verb *To be*

It's cool.
It's fifty degrees.

It 's raining now.

It 's going to rain tomorrow.

PRACTICE

Fill in the blanks with the correct tense. Read the entire weather report before you begin. Use contractions whenever possible.

This is the weather report for today–Wednesday, October 23.

It _'s_____ warm and sunny here with a temperature of 70 degrees, but
(1. be)

right now clouds _____ our way. There's a chance of rain
(2. move)

later today. In the mountains the temperature _____ 50 degrees, and
(3. be)

it _____ right now. The weather _____ cool.
(4. rain)   (5. be)

Tomorrow it _____ here. In the afternoon
(6. rain)

it _____ windy, and the temperature _____ 40
(7. be)   (8. be)

degrees. In the mountains it _____ cold tomorrow.
(9. get)

It _____ 20 to 30 degrees, and it _____ .
(10. be)   (11. snow)

You _____ warm coats and umbrellas for tomorrow, folks.
(12. need)

This is Bell Snow reporting for Channel 30.

78

THE POST OFFICE IS ACROSS FROM THE POLICE STATION.

Prepositions of Place: *Next To, Across From, Between, On*

Verb *To Be*

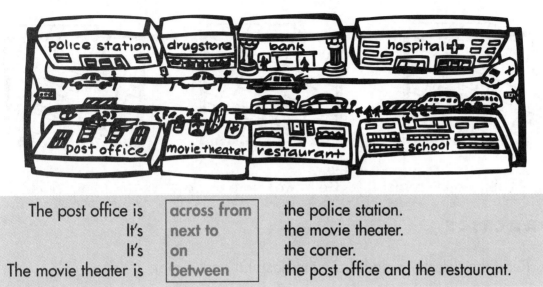

The post office is	across from	the police station.
It's	next to	the movie theater.
It's	on	the corner.
The movie theater is	between	the post office and the restaurant.

PRACTICE

Look at the picture above. Then fill in the blanks with *next to*, *across from*, *between*, or *on*.

Where's the police station?   1. It's ___*on*___ the corner.

2. It's _____ the post office.

3. It's _____ the drugstore.

Where's the drugstore?   4. It's _____ the movie theater.

5. It's _____ the police station and the bank.

Where's the bank?   6. It's _____ the drugstore.

7. It's _____ the drugstore and the hospital.

Where's the hospital?   8. It's _____ the bank.

9. It's _____ the corner.

10. It's _____ the school.

Where's the school?   11. It's _____ the restaurant.

12. It's _____ the corner.

WALK TO THE CORNER.

Affirmative Statements

Imperatives

| Walk | to the corner. | Go | two more blocks. | Turn | right. |

PRACTICE

A. Read the directions and draw the hospital on the map.

Walk to the corner.
Turn left.
Go two blocks.
Turn right.
Look for the sign.
Walk to the corner.
The hospital is on the corner.

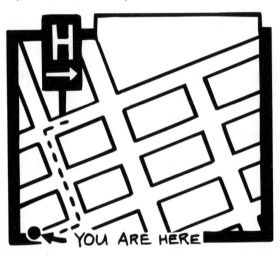

B. Now tell someone how to get to the bus stop.

■ Excuse me. Where's the bus stop?

☐ 1. *Walk to the corner.*

2. _____

3. _____

4. _____

5. _____

6. _____

7. _____

■ Thanks.

☐ You're welcome.

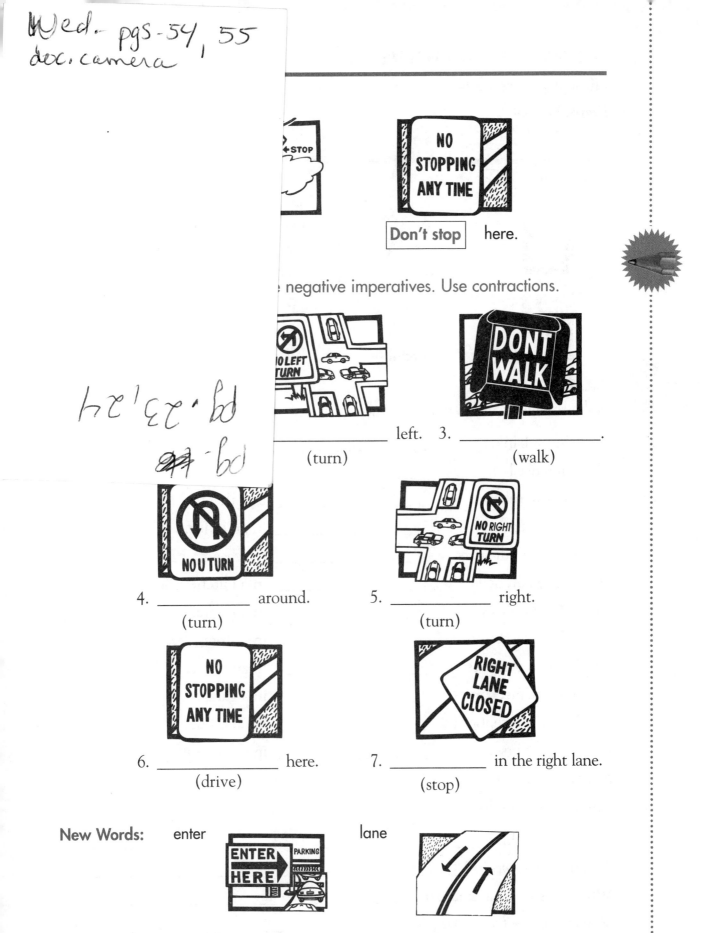

+STOP

NO
STOPPING
ANY TIME

Don't stop   here.

negative imperatives. Use contractions.

_____ left.   3. _____.
(turn)   (walk)

4. _____ around.   5. _____ right.
(turn)   (turn)

6. _____ here.   7. _____ in the right lane.
(drive)   (stop)

New Words: enter   lane

SHE WORKS IN A HOSPITAL.

Affirmative Statements

Simple Present

| I
You
We | work | in a hospital. | He
She | works | in a hospital. |

theater   school   beauty parlor   butcher shop

restaurant   hospital   bank   garage

PRACTICE

Make sentences with *work* or *works*.

1. She's a banker.   _She works_   in a bank.
2. I'm a teacher.   _____   in a school.
3. They're ushers.   _____   in a theater.
4. He's a dentist.   _____   in an office.
5. We're hairdressers.   _____   in a beauty parlor.
6. You're butchers.   _____   in a butcher shop.
7. She's a waitress.   _____   in a restaurant.
8. I'm a salesperson.   _____   in a store.
9. We're secretaries.   _____   in an office.
10. They're mechanics.   _____   in a garage.
11. You're a receptionist   _____   in an office.
12. She's a nurse.   _____   in a hospital.

MAKE IT WORK

Answer the questions.

What do you do? _____

Where do you work? _____

What does your classmate do? _____

Where does he (or she) work? _____

AFTER DINNER, HE RELAXES ON THE COUCH.

Spelling: *-s, -es, -ies*

Simple Present

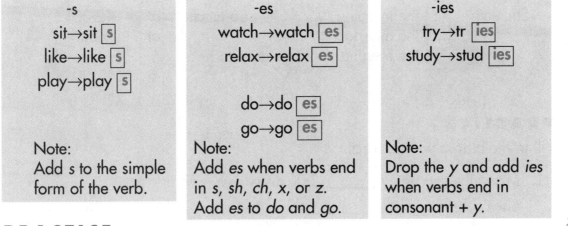

-s	-es	-ies
sit→sit s	watch→watch es	try→tr ies
like→like s	relax→relax es	study→stud ies
play→play s		
	do→do es	
	go→go es	
Note: Add *s* to the simple form of the verb.	**Note:** Add *es* when verbs end in *s, sh, ch, x,* or *z*. Add *es* to *do* and *go*.	**Note:** Drop the *y* and add *ies* when verbs end in consonant + *y*.

PRACTICE

Fill in the blanks with the correct form of the verb. (Felix is a cat.)

1. (get) Felix ___*gets*___ up at 7:00 every morning.

2. (stand) He _____ next to his dish in the kitchen.

3. (wait) He _____ for his breakfast.

4. (like) He _____ meat for breakfast.

5. (go) After breakfast, he _____ outside.

6. (play) He _____ in the yard.

7. (watch/try) He _____ the birds, but he never _____ to run after them.

8. (chase/catch) He _____ butterflies, but he never _____ them.

9. (come) At 10:00, he _____ into the house.

10. (drink) He _____ some milk.

11. (sit/wash) He _____ on the bed and _____ himself.

12. (go) In the afternoon, he _____ outside.

13. (eat) At 5:30, he _____ his dinner.

14. (relax/sleep) After dinner, he _____ on the couch and _____.

New Words: bird   butterfly   chase   catch

SHE USUALLY GOES TO BED AT MIDNIGHT.

Prepositions of Time: *In* and *At*

Simple Present

She eats	in	the morning.	She eats lunch	at	12:00.
	in	the afternoon.		at	noon.
	in	the evening.	She goes to bed	at	night.
				at	11:00.
				at	midnight.

PRACTICE

Fill in the blanks with *in* or *at*.

1. Mrs. Alba gets up __*at*__ 7:00 every day.
2. She cooks breakfast _____ the morning.
3. Mr. Alba goes to work _____ 8:00.
4. _____ 8:15, Mrs. Alba washes the dishes.
5. She cleans the house _____ the morning.
6. _____ noon, she eats lunch.
7. _____ the afternoon, she washes or irons.
8. _____ 5:00, she watches the news on television.
9. She cooks dinner _____ 5:30.
10. Mr. Alba comes home _____ 6:00 or 6:30.
11. Mr. and Mrs. Alba eat dinner _____ 7:00.
12. Mrs. Alba watches television _____ the evening.
13. She goes to bed very late _____ night.
14. She usually goes to bed _____ midnight.

MAKE IT WORK

Answer the questions.

What time do you get up?_____

What time do you go to bed? _____

What time do you eat breakfast? _____

What time do you eat lunch? _____

What time do you eat dinner? _____

New Words: noon   midnight

HE NEVER DRINKS WINE.

Adverbs of Frequency

Simple Present

He drinks milk.	He	always	drinks milk.
He drinks wine.	He	never	drinks wine.

Note: Words like *always, usually, often, sometimes, rarely,* and *never* come before the main verb in most cases. *Never* expresses a negative idea.

PRACTICE

Add the adverbs to the sentences.

1. He gets up early. (always)

   He always gets up early.

2. He exercises. (always)

   _____

3. He exercises for two hours. (often)

   _____

4. For breakfast, he drinks coffee. (never)

   _____

5. He drinks milk. (always)

   _____

6. He eats too much. (rarely)

   _____

7. He smokes cigarettes. (never)

   _____

8. He drinks wine. (never)

   _____

9. He sleeps eight hours at night. (usually)

   _____

10. He sleeps nine or ten hours at night. (sometimes)

    _____

MAKE IT WORK

Check the appropriate boxes.

Health Checklist

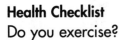

Do you exercise?	Do you sleep eight hours at night?	Do you take vitamins?
☐ always	☐ always	☐ always
☐ never	☐ never	☐ never
☐ sometimes	☐ sometimes	☐ sometimes

I HAVE A HEADACHE.

Affirmative Statements: *Have* and *Has*

Simple Present

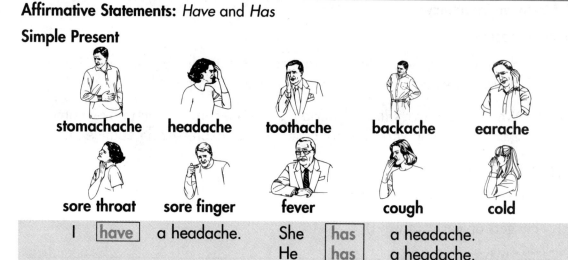

stomachache	headache	toothache	backache	earache
sore throat	sore finger	fever	cough	cold

I	have	a headache.	She	has	a headache.
			He	has	a headache.

PRACTICE

Make sentences with *have* or *has*.

1. What's the matter with you? (stomachache) *I have a stomachache.*

2. What's the matter with Gloria? (headache) _____

3. What's the matter with Carlo? (toothache) _____

4. What's the matter with Oscar? (backache) _____

5. What's the matter with you? (earache) _____

6. What's the matter with Julia? (sore throat) _____

7. What's the matter with you? (sore finger) _____

8. What's the matter with Chang? (fever) _____

9. What's the matter with you? (cough) _____

10. What's the matter with Marie? (cold) _____

MAKE IT WORK

Look at the picture. Then fill in the dialogue.

■ What's the matter with you, Gloria?

☐ _____

■ I'm sorry to hear that.

YOU HAVE A BIG FAMILY.

Affirmative Statements: *Have* and *Has*

Simple Present

I	**have**	a big family.	She	**has**	a big family.
You	**have**	a big family.	He	**has**	a big family.
They	**have**	a big family.			

PRACTICE

Fill in the blanks with *have* or *has*.

■ Are you married?

☐ Yes, I am. I ___have___ two children—a son and a daughter. Here's
(1)
a picture of my daughter. She _____ two children.
(2)

■ She looks very young.

☐ She's 28.

■ And what about your son?

☐ He's married, and he _____ a new baby girl. So I'm a
(3)
grandmother. I _____ three grandchildren.
(4)

■ You _____ a big family.
(5)

☐ What about you?

■ I'm not married. I live with my sister and her husband. They
_____ two children. I _____ a brother in Colombia. He
(6) (7)
_____ five children—all boys.
(8)

☐ You _____ a big family, too.
(9)

■ Yes, I do. I _____ a picture of my brother and his family.
(10)
Do you want to see it?

MAKE IT WORK

Tell about your family.

_____

_____

_____

SHE LOVES ANIMALS.

Affirmative Statements: *-s, -es*

Simple Present

Carlo Alba

I like my job at the bank. The hours are long, but the pay is good. I live in an apartment two blocks from the bank, and I walk to work.

Anna Thanos

I go to school, and I also have a part-time job. I work in my parents restaurant at night. I live with my parents in a house.

Rafael Moreno

I'm a construction worker. It's a tough job, but I need the money. I have four children.

Julia Santos

I work in a department store. I live in a house with a big yard because I have a lot of pets. I love animals. I have four dogs and three cats.

SHE LOVES ANIMALS.

> I go to school, and I also have a part-time job.
> She │ goes │ to school, and she also │ has │ a part-time job.

PRACTICE

Read page 88. Then make affirmative sentences about the people in the pictures.

1. (work)   Carlo Alba _works in a bank._
2. (like)   He _____
3. (live)   He _____
4. (walk)   He _____
5. (go)   Anna Thanos _____
6. (have)   She _____
7. (work)   She _____
8. (live)   She _____
9. (be)   Rafael Moreno _____
10. (have)   He _____
11. (work)   Julia Santos_____
12. (live)   She _____
13. (love)   She _____
14. (have)   She _____

MAKE IT WORK

Tell where you work and live.

_____

_____

_____

New Words:    dog

pet = an animal who lives with people,
     like a dog or a cat

tough = hard or difficult

89

SHE HAS TWO FULL-TIME JOBS.

Affirmative Statements: *-s, -es*

Simple Present

I	get	up at 5:30.
She	gets	up at 5:30.

Note: Use the present tense for actions that happen every day.

PRACTICE

Read what Rosa Camino says about her day. Then rewrite the sentences. Tell about *Rosa*. Change *I* to *she* and *my* to *her*.

I have two full-time jobs. I work in a hospital, and I take care of my family. I get up at 5:30 every morning. I cook breakfast for my son and my husband. At 6:30 I get my son, Paco, ready for school. At 7:00 I drive Paco to school. I get to the hospital at 7:30. I work from 7:30 to 3:30. After work I pick Paco up at school. I go home, and I cook dinner. After dinner I do the dishes. On Wednesday evening, I go to class. After class, I make lunch for my husband and my son. I sometimes watch television in the evening if I'm not too tired. I usually go to bed at 10:30.

Rosa Camino has two full-time jobs. She _____

_____

_____

_____

_____

_____

_____

_____

_____

_____

_____

_____

_____

_____

New Word: full-time job = work that is eight hours a day, five days a week

DO YOU HAVE ANY BROTHERS AND SISTERS?

Yes-No Questions

Simple Present

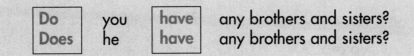

Do	you	have	any brothers and sisters?
Does	he	have	any brothers and sisters?

PRACTICE

Look at the chart. Then write some questions you would like to ask a classmate.

Do Does	you your husband your wife your children your brother(s) your sister(s)	have live work like go	any brothers and sisters? any children? with you? at night? your job? any pets in an apartment? in a house? to school?

1. _Do you work?_ _____

2. _____

3. _____

4. _____

5. _____

6. _____

7. _____

8. _____

9. _____

10. _____

MAKE IT WORK

Interview a classmate, using the questions above. Then write two sentences about your classmate.

_____

_____

DOES HE GET UP AT 9:00?

Yes-No Questions

Simple Present

He   gets   up at 9:00.   They   get   up at 9:00.

| Does | he | get | up at 9:00? | | Do | they | get | up at 9:00? |

PRACTICE

Make questions.

1. Mr. Gross and Mr. Tong are neighbors.

   Are Mr. Gross and Mr. Tong neighbors?

2. They live in the same apartment building.

   Do they live in the same apartment building?

3. They live in Los Angeles.

4. They do the same thing every evening.

5. They get up at 9:00 at night.

6. They go to work at 10:00.

7. They work from 11:00 to 7:00.

8. They come home from work in the morning.

9. Mr. Gross goes to bed at 1:00 P.M.

10. Mr. Tong goes to bed at 2:00.

11. Mr. Tong is a night watchman.

12. He watches buildings at night.

13. He works for a construction company.

14. Mr. Gross is a night watchman, too.

15. He works for a movie studio.

DO THEY LIVE IN LOS ANGELES? YES, THEY DO.

Negative and Affirmative Short Answers

Simple Present

Do Mr. Gross and Mr. Tong live in New York?	No, they don't.
Do they live in Los Angeles?	Yes, they do.
Does Mr. Gross work in New York?	No, he doesn't.
Does he work in Los Angeles?	Yes, he does.

PRACTICE

Look at the information on page 92. Then answer the questions below. Use short answers.

1. Are Mr. Tong and Mr. Gross neighbors?   *Yes, they are.*

2. Do they live in the same apartment
   building?   *Yes, they do.*

3. Do they live in Los Angeles?   _____

4. Do they get up at 7:00 at night?   _____

5. Do they get up at 9:00 at night?   _____

6. Do they work from 9:00 to 5:00?   _____

7. Do they work from 11:00 to 7:00?   _____

8. Do they come home from work in the
   evening?   _____

9. Is Mr. Tong a night watchman?   _____

10. Does he watch buildings?   _____

11. Does he work for a movie studio?   _____

12. Does he work for a construction company?   _____

13. Is Mr. Gross a night watchman?   _____

14. Does he work at night?   _____

15. Does he work for a bank?   _____

MAKE IT WORK

Answer the questions.

Do you work? _____

Do you work at night? _____

THEY DON'T WORK IN THE DAYTIME.

Negative Statements

Simple Present

He	gets	up in the morning.
He	doesn't get	up in the morning.
They	get	up in the morning.
They	don't get	up in the morning.

contractions: doesn't = does not   don't = do not

P R A C T I C E

Make the sentences negative.

1. Mr. Gross and Mr. Tong get up in the morning.   *Mr. Gross and Mr. Tong don't get up in the morning.*

2. They have breakfast in the morning.   _____

3. They go to work at 8:00.   _____

4. They get to work at 9:00.   _____

5. They work from 9:00 to 5:00.   _____

6. They come home in the evening.   _____

7. Mr. Tong eats dinner in the evening.   _____

8. He relaxes at night.   _____

9. He watches television.   _____

10. He goes to bed at 11:00 at night.   _____

11. Mr. Gross reads at night.   _____

12. He goes to bed at midnight.   _____

13. Mr. Tong and Mr. Gross sleep at night.   _____

14. They work in the daytime.   _____

15. Night watchmen watch buildings in the daytime.   _____

SHE DOESN'T MAKE A LOT OF MONEY.

Negative Statements

Simple Present

Marie Moore		lives	in Beverly Hills.
Katie Anders	doesn't	live	in Beverly Hills.
Katie Anders and her husband	don't	live	in Beverly Hills.

PRACTICE

Read the sentences below. Then make the sentences negative. Change Marie to Katie. Use contractions.

Marie Moore is a famous actress. She makes a lot of money. She and her husband live in a big house in Beverly Hills. They have a private movie theater in their house. Marie drives a Rolls Royce. She wears expensive clothes. She has a lot of beautiful jewelry. She and her husband give a lot of big parties. They own an airplane. They travel to Spain for their vacations. Marie has it all.

Katie Anders isn't a famous actress. She _____

_____

_____

_____

_____

_____

_____

_____

_____

MAKE IT WORK

Make one negative sentence about your life.

_____

New Words: own = possess

jewelry

airplane

95

WHO HAS MY KEYS? I HAVE THEM.

Object Pronouns: *Them* and *It*

Simple Present

Who has my keys?	I have	them.
Who has my pencil?	Gloria has	it.

Note: Object pronouns are often used after verbs.

noun	pronoun
keys	them
pencil	it

PRACTICE

Make sentences with *have* or *has* and *it* or *them*.

1. Who has my keys?   I _have them._

2. Who has my glasses?   Anna _____

3. Who has my camera?   Gloria and Oscar_____

4. Who has my umbrella?   Mohsen _____

5. Who has my books?   I _____

6. Who has my pen?   Julia_____

7. Who has my wallet?   You _____

8. Who has my papers?   The teacher_____

9. Who has my dictionary?   We _____

10. Who has my tennis racket?   Loi _____

11. Who has my gloves?   I _____

12. Who has my registration form?   Chang _____

MAKE IT WORK

Fill in the blanks with the correct pronouns.

■ Who has my keys?

☐ I have _____. _____ are right here.

PLEASE HELP ME.

Object Pronouns

Simple Present, Imperatives

I need some help.	Please help	me.
He needs some help.	Please help	him.
She needs some help.	Please help	her.
We need some help.	Please help	us.
They need some help.	Please help	them.

noun	subject pronoun	object pronoun
Oscar	he	him
Oscar and Gloria	they	them
Oscar and I	we	us

PRACTICE

Fill in the blanks with the correct object pronoun.

1. I need some help. Please help _me_.

2. Oscar and Gloria need some help. Please help _____.

3. We need some help. Please help _____.

4. Louise needs some help. Please help _____.

5. I need some help. Please help _____.

6. Mohsen needs some help. Please help _____.

7. They need some help. Please help _____.

8. Loi and I need some help. Please help _____.

9. Julia needs some help. Please help _____.

10. Akira needs some help. Please help _____.

11. Louise and Raymond need some help. Please help _____.

12. Florie and I need some help. Please help _____.

MAKE IT WORK

What is the woman in the picture saying?
Fill in the blank.

_____

I SEE HIM, BUT HE DOESN'T SEE ME.

Object and Subject Pronouns

Simple Present

I	see	him,	but	he	doesn't see	me.
You	see	me,	but	I	don't see	you.
He	sees	her,	but	she	doesn't see	him.
She	sees	us,	but	we	don't see	her.
We	see	them,	but	they	don't see	us.
They	see	you,	but	you	doesn't see	them.

PRACTICE

Complete these sentences with a negative and the correct pronouns.

1. I know him, but *he doesn't know me.* _____

2. He knows me, but _____

3. We knows her, but_____

4. You see him, but _____

5. They see us, but_____

6. We see them, but _____

7. She hears me, but _____

8. I hear you, but _____

9. He hears me, but _____

10. I understand him, but _____

11. They understand you, but _____

12. You understand us, but _____

MAKE IT WORK

Look at the picture. Then fill in the blanks with pronouns.

_____ sees _____, but

_____ doesn't see _____.

SHE LIVES ON PARK AVENUE.

Prepositions of Place: *In, On, At*

Simple Present

She lives	in	New York.
She lives	on	Park Avenue.
She lives	at	1142 Park Avenue.

Note: Use *in* for cities, towns, countries.
　　　Use *on* for streets, roads, avenues, boulevards, drives.
　　　Use *at* for *address*.

PRACTICE

Fill in the blanks with *in, on,* or *at.*

1. She lives __*on*__ Pacific Avenue.

2. She lives _____ San Francisco.

3. She works _____ 23 Market Street.

4. They live _____ Los Angeles.

5. They live _____ 1592 Flower Street.

6. They work _____ Hollywood Boulevard.

7. We live _____ Hollywood.

8. We live _____ Sunset Boulevard.

9. We live _____ 1171 Sunset Boulevard.

10. He works _____ New York.

11. He works _____ 102 Park Avenue.

12. He lives _____ Madison Avenue.

13. You live _____ Miami Beach.

14. You live _____ Atlantic Road.

15. I live _____ 556 Lakeshore Drive.

16. I live _____ Chicago.

MAKE IT WORK

Answer the questions.

What street do you live on? _____

What number do you live at? _____

What city do you live in? _____

What country do you live in? _____

WHERE IN LOS ANGELES DO YOU LIVE?

Questions with *Where*

Simple Present

> I live in Los Angeles.
>
> [Where] in Los Angeles do you live?
>
> I live on Doheny Drive.
>
> [Where] on Doheny Drive do you live?

PRACTICE

Make questions with *where.*

1. He lives in Los Angeles.   *Where in Los Angeles does he live?*
2. He lives on Flower Street.   _____
3. He works in Hollywood.   _____
4. He works on Doheny Drive.   _____

5. They live in New York.   _____
6. They live on Park Avenue.   _____
7. I work in San Francisco.   _____
8. I work on Market Street.   _____
9. She lives in Miami Beach.   _____
10. She lives on Atlantic Road. _____
11. We work in Chicago.   _____
12. We work on Lakeshore Drive. _____

MAKE IT WORK

Make questions with *where.*

■ _____?

☐ I work on Park Avenue.

■ I work on Park Avenue, too. _____?

☐ At 102 Park Avenue.

■ I work at 53 Park Avenue.

WHAT DOES HE DO?

Questions with *What* and *Where*

Simple Present

What	does he do?	He's an office manager.
Where	does he work?	He works in Los Angeles.
What company	does he work for?	He works for ABC Company.

PRACTICE

Look at the business cards. Then make questions with *what*, *where*, and *what company*. Answer your questions.

Thomas Turner

A T T O R N E Y - A T - L A W

Turner and Turner
500 Fifth Ave.
New York, NY 10025
(212) 555-LAWS

1. *What does he do?*

   He's an attorney.

2. _____

   _____

3. _____

   _____

Gloria Sanchez   Interior Decorator

Home Interiors

5116 Sunset Boulevard
Los Angeles, CA 90069
Business: (213) 555-1111

4. _____

   _____

5. _____

   _____

6. _____

J.G.S. MEDICAL GROUP

Jan Sola, M.D.
George Porter, M.D.

2400 Lake Drive
Chicago, IL.
(312) 555-7000

MEDICAL GROUP

7. _____

   _____

8. _____

   _____

9. _____

   _____

New Words: M.D. = medical doctor   attorney = lawyer

CHRISTA'S MOTHER TAKES CARE OF THEIR SON.

Review: Simple Present

Chuck and Christa	work.	
Christa's mother	takes	care of their son.

PRACTICE

Fill in the blanks with the correct form of the verb.

Chuck and Christa _____ a son, Mike, who is 13 months
(1. have)

old. Chuck and Christa _____ from 9:00 to 5:00, so Christa's
(2. work)

mother Helga, _____ care of Mike in the daytime.
(3. take)

It _____ a hard job to take care of a small baby. Helga
(4. be)

_____ busy all day. Mike _____ up at 6:00 in the
(5. be)   (6. wake)

morning. He _____ breakfast at 6:30. After breakfast Helga
(7. eat)

usually _____ to Mike. At 10:00 he _____ a nap.
(8. read)   (9. take)

Before he goes to sleep, he usually _____ some juice. He
(10. drink)

_____ up from his nap at around 12:00. He _____
(11. get)   (12. have)

lunch right away. In the afternoon Helga and Mike _____ to the
(13. go)

park. Mike _____ a nap in the afternoon, and at 5:00 he usually
(14. take)

_____ dinner.
(15. eat)

Chuck and Christa _____ home at 6:00. They
(16. get)

_____ dinner at 7:00. In the evening they _____
(17. have)   (18. play)

with Mike and they _____ television. Mike _____
(19. watch)   (20. go)

to bed at 9:00 P.M. By then Helga, Chuck, and Christa _____
(21. be)

exhausted. They _____ to bed at 9:30.
(22. go)

New Words: exhausted = very tired   nap = short sleep

CHUCK AND CHRISTA WATCH TV EVERY NIGHT. THEY'RE WATCHING TV NOW.

Contrast: Present vs. Present Continuous

| Chuck and Christa | watch | TV every night. |
| They | 're watching | TV now. |

PRACTICE

Look at the picture above. Then fill in the blanks with the correct tense. Use contractions whenever possible.

1. (work) Chuck and Christa __work__ from 9:00 to 5:00 every day.

2. (work) Chuck _____ in a bank.

3. (work) Christa _____ in an office.

4. (relax) Right now they _____.

5. (play) They _____ with Mike now.

6. (play) They _____ with Mike every night after dinner.

7. (watch) They also _____ TV every night.

8. (watch) They _____ TV now.

9. (watch) Helga _____ TV with Chuck and Christa every night.

10. (sleep) Right now she _____.

11. (fall) She _____ asleep in front of the TV almost every night.

12. (play) Mike _____ with his parents now.

13. (go) He _____ to bed at 9:00.

14. (go) His parents _____ to bed at 9:30.

MAKE IT WORK

Tell about yourself.

I _____ an ESL student.

_____ English every day.

_____ English now.

New Words: TV = television

IT'S USUALLY COOL IN THE FALL.

Contrast: Adverbs of Frequency with the Present
Verb *To Be*, Simple Present

summer   fall   winter   spring

often

It's cold.   It snows in the winter.

Note: In most cases adverbs of frequency go after the *verb to be* and before other main verbs.

PRACTICE

Add the adverbs to the sentences.

1. It's hot in the summer. (always)

   It's always hot in the summer.

2. It snows in the summer. (never)

   _____

3. It rains in the summer. (sometimes)

   _____

4. It's cool in the fall. (usually)

   _____

5. It rains in the fall. (sometimes)

   _____

6. It snows in the winter. (usually)

   _____

7. It's cold in the winter. (always)

   _____

8. It rains a lot in the spring. (usually)

   _____

9. It's warm in the spring. (often)

   _____

10. It snows in the spring. (rarely)

    _____

IT ALWAYS SNOWS IN THE WINTER. IT'S SNOWING NOW.

Contrast: Present vs. Present Continuous

| It always | snows | in the winter. |
| It | 's snowing | now. |

PRACTICE

Fill in the blanks with the correct tense. Use contractions whenever possible.

1. (rain) It _'s raining_____ now.

2. (wear) People _____ raincoats.

3. (rain) It sometimes _____ in the summer.

4. (wear) When it rains, people usually _____ raincoats.

5. (snow) It _____ today.

6. (wear) People _____ heavy coats today.

7. (snow) It always _____ in the winter.

8. (wear) People _____ heavy coats in the winter.

9. (be) It _____ very hot today.

10. (wear) People _____ shorts and T-shirts.

11. (wear) In the summer, people usually _____ light clothing.

12. (be) It _____ very windy and cool today.

13. (wear) People _____ sweaters and jackets when it's cool and windy.

14. (wear) People usually _____ sweaters and jackets when it's cool and windy.

15. (wear) People usually _____ sweaters and jackets in the fall and spring.

MAKE IT WORK

Answer the questions.

What season is it now? _____

What are people wearing today? _____

What season is usually cold? _____

What do people usually wear when it's cold? _____

_____

SHE CAN PLAY THE PIANO VERY WELL.

Affirmative Statements

Can

I			
He	can play	the piano.	She
They			

She can play the piano very well.

PRACTICE

Make new sentences with *can*.

1. Andy can swim.   In fact, *he can swim very well.*
2. Brian and Carmen can ski.   In fact, _____
3. Carmen can ice-skate.   In fact, _____
4. Linda can ride a bicycle.   In fact, _____
5. Brian and Carmen can
   play golf.   In fact, _____
6. Andy can play baseball.   In fact, _____
7. Carmen can play the piano.   In fact, _____
8. Brian and Carmen can dance. In fact, _____
9. Brian can play the guitar.   In fact, _____
10. Carmen can play tennis.   In fact, _____
11. Brian and Carmen can
    play chess.   In fact, _____
12. Brian can cook.   In fact, _____

MAKE IT WORK

Answer the question.

What can you do very well? _____

_____

New Words: ice-skate   ski

Note: Use *in fact* to say something in a stronger way.

106

SHE CAN'T DANCE.

Negative Statements

Can

She can lift sixty pounds.
contraction: can't = cannot

He can't lift sixty pounds.

PRACTICE

Make sentences with *can't.*

1. *She can't dance.*

2. _____

3. _____

4. _____

5. _____

6. _____

MAKE IT WORK

Answer the question.

What can't you do very well? _____

_____

THESE SHOES ARE TOO NARROW.

Too and *Very*

Can

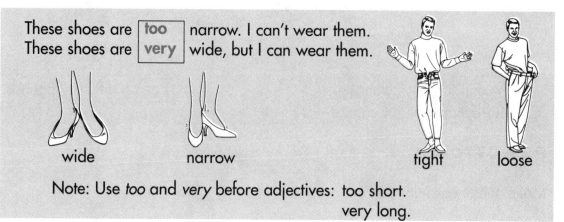

These shoes are | too | narrow. I can't wear them.
These shoes are | very | wide, but I can wear them.

wide   narrow   tight   loose

Note: Use *too* and *very* before adjectives: too short.
                                              very long.

PRACTICE

Fill in the blanks with *too* or *very*.

1. This blouse is _*too*_____ small. I can't wear it.

2. This skirt is _____ short, but I can wear it.

3. This dress is _____ big. I can't wear it.

4. These shoes are _____ long, but I can wear them.

5. These shoes are _____ narrow. I can't wear them.

6. This belt is _____ short. I can't wear it.

7. This hat is _____ small. I can't wear it.

8. These pants are _____ long, but I can wear them.

9. These pants are _____ tight. I can't wear them.

10. These pants are _____ loose. I can't wear them.

11. This shirt is _____ big, but I can wear it.

12. These gloves are _____ tight. I can't wear them.

MAKE IT WORK

Look at the picture and tell what's wrong.

_____

_____

_____

IT'S TOO HEAVY.

Too and *Very*

Can

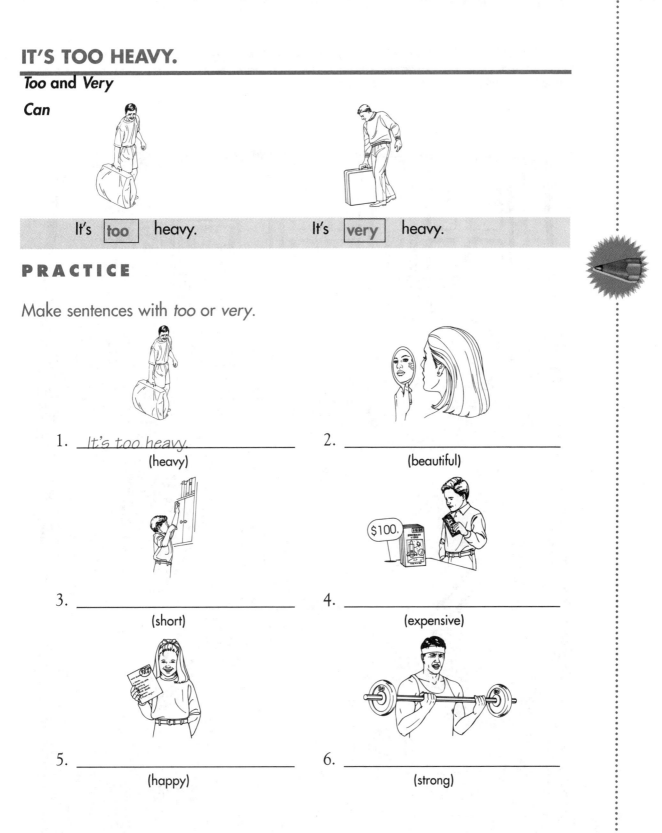

It's | too | heavy.   It's | very | heavy.

PRACTICE

Make sentences with *too* or *very*.

1. _It's too heavy._
   (heavy)

2. _____
   (beautiful)

3. _____
   (short)

4. _____
   (expensive)

5. _____
   (happy)

6. _____
   (strong)

MAKE IT WORK

Fill in the blanks. Tell about yourself.

I'm too _____.

I'm very_____.

109

CAN YOU LIFT THE COUCH? NO, I CAN'T.

Negative and Affirmative Short Answers

Can

CAN YOU LIFT THE COUCH? NO, I CAN'T.

Can you lift the couch?	No, I can't.
Can you carry the end table?	Yes, I can.

PRACTICE

Look at the picture on page 110. Then answer the questions with short answers. Tell about yourself.

No, I can't.

1. Can you lift the bookcase? _____
2. Can you lift the couch? _____
3. Can you lift the coffee table? _____
4. Can you lift the armchair? _____
5. Can you lift the end table? _____
6. Can you lift the piano? _____
7. Can you lift the lamp? _____
8. Can you carry the lamp? _____
9. Can you carry the couch? _____
10. Can you carry the large plant? _____
11. Can you carry the stereo? _____
12. Can you carry the box? _____
13. Can you carry the armchair? _____
14. Can you carry the rug? _____

MAKE IT WORK

Answer the questions.

Can you type? _____

Can you type 100 words a minute? _____

Can you run? _____

Can you run a mile in five minutes? _____

Equivalent: .62 mile = one kilometer

I CAN'T MOVE THIS BOX. CAN YOU MOVE IT?

Yes-No Questions

Can

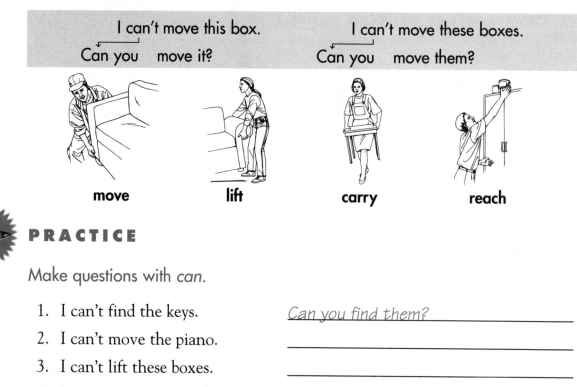

I can't move this box.	I can't move these boxes.
Can you move it?	Can you move them?

| move | lift | carry | reach |

PRACTICE

Make questions with *can*.

1. I can't find the keys.   *Can you find them?*
2. I can't move the piano.   _____
3. I can't lift these boxes.   _____
4. I can't open this window.   _____
5. I can't close this drawer.   _____
6. I can't carry these pictures.   _____
7. I can't reach the top shelf.   _____
8. I can't lift these plants.   _____
9. I can't find the dictionary.   _____
10. I can't carry these books.   _____

MAKE IT WORK

Look at the pictures. Then ask a classmate two questions with *can*.

_____

_____

Equivalent: one pound = .45 kilogram

I CAN SKI BUT NOT VERY WELL.

Review: *Can*

I	can't	ice-skate.
I	can	ski but not very well.
I	can	play tennis very well.

PRACTICE

A. Look at the list below. Then name some things you can't do at all. Use contractions.

ice-skate	play the piano	sing
play tennis	play the guitar	draw
play golf	play chess	cook
play soccer	drive a car	dance
ski	ride a bicycle	

1. *I can't ice-skate.* _____
2. _____
3. _____
4. _____
5. _____

B. Look at the list again. Now name some things you can do, telling how well you can do each one.

6. *I can swim but not very well. OR I can swim very well.* _____
7. _____
8. _____
9. _____
10. _____

MAKE IT WORK

Tell how well you can do the following things.

speak English _____

understand English _____

write English _____

read English _____

THE BEACHES WERE BEAUTIFUL.

Affirmative Statements

Past of Verb *To Be*

> John was in Puerto Rico last week.
> The weather | was | warm.
> The beaches | were | beautiful.
>
> Note: Use the past tense for actions that happened yesterday, last week, last month.

PRACTICE

Fill in the blanks with *was* or *were*.

1. John _was_ in Puerto Rico last week.

2. He _____ there for five days.

3. Puerto Rico _____ beautiful.

4. The beaches _____ nice.

5. Old San Juan _____ interesting.

6. The old churches _____ beautiful.

7. The restaurants in Puerto Rico _____ excellent.

8. The people _____ friendly.

9. The weather _____ warm and sunny all week.

10. John's hotel _____ modern.

11. His hotel room _____ very clean.

12. All in all, it _____ a wonderful trip.

MAKE IT WORK

Tell about your last trip to a city.

Was it a good trip? a wonderful trip? a terrible trip?
Was the city beautiful? interesting? boring?
Was the weather nice? warm? sunny? cloudy? cold?
Were the restaurants good? excellent? fair? bad? expensive?
Were the people friendly? helpful? nice? rude?

I was in _____. It was a _____

trip. The city _____

_____

_____

_____

THE WEATHER WASN'T NICE.

Negative Statements

Past of Verb *To Be*

The weather	was	nice.		The beaches	were	nice.
The weather	wasn't	nice.		The beaches	weren't	nice.

contractions: wasn't = was not   weren't = were not

PRACTICE

Tell about Marie's vacation. Make negative sentences. Use contractions.

John was on vacation last week.	Marie was on vacation last week.
1. John's vacation was interesting.	*Marie's vacation wasn't interesting.*
2. The beaches were nice.	_____
3. They were clean.	_____
4. The bus tour was interesting.	_____
5. The city was very pretty.	_____
6. The restaurants were very good.	_____
7. The people were friendly.	_____
8. They were very helpful.	_____
9. The weather was nice.	_____
10. It was warm and sunny.	_____
11. John's hotel was large.	_____
12. It was new and modern.	_____
13. It was on the beach.	_____
14. His room was very clean.	_____

MAKE IT WORK

Name three negative things about your last vacation.

_____

_____

_____

WAS IT SUNNY?

Yes-No Questions
Past of Verb *To Be*

The weather was nice.	The beaches were beautiful.
Was it sunny?	Were they clean?

PRACTICE

Make questions.

The beaches were beautiful.

1. (clean) *Were they clean?*
2. (safe) _____
3. (crowded) _____

The restaurants were good.

4. (expensive) _____

_____

The weather was nice.

5. (sunny) _____
6. (warm) _____
7. (hot) _____

The people were nice.

8. (helpful) _____
9. (friendly) _____

The hotel was large.

10. (modern) _____
11. (old) _____
12. (on the beach) _____

_____

13. (near the beach) _____

_____

The hotel rooms were clean.

14. (large) _____
15. (expensive) _____

_____

The bus tour was expensive.

16. (interesting) _____

_____

WERE MARIA AND PEDRO AT THE MOVIES? NO, THEY WEREN'T.

Negative and Affirmative Short Answers

Past of Verb *To Be*

Oscar

Gloria

Alfonso, Pedro, Maria

Was Oscar at church yesterday?	No, he wasn't.
Was Oscar at school yesterday?	Yes, he was.
Were Maria and Pedro at the movies?	No, they weren't.
Were Maria and Pedro at the zoo?	Yes, they were.

PRACTICE

Look at the pictures above. Then answer the questions with short answers.

1. Was Oscar at work yesterday? *No, he wasn't.*

2. Was Oscar at school? _____

3. Was Gloria at school? _____

4. Was Gloria at the laundromat? _____

5. Was Alfonso at the laundromat? _____

6. Was Alfonso at the zoo? _____

7. Was Maria at the movies? _____

8. Were Alfonso and Maria at the movies? _____

9. Were Alfonso and Maria at the zoo? _____

10. Was Pedro at the zoo? _____

11. Were Pedro, Alfonso, and Maria at the zoo? _____

12. Were Oscar and Gloria at the zoo? _____

MAKE IT WORK

Answer the questions.

Were you at home yesterday? _____

Were you at work? _____

WE WERE AT SCHOOL.

No Article with *Home, Church, School, Work*

Past of Verb *To Be*

I		at	the	store.
He	was	at	the	movies.
She		at	the	zoo.
You		at		home.
We	were	at		school.
They		at		work.
		at		church.

Note: Do not use *the* with *at home, at school, at work,* or *at church.*

PRACTICE

Answer the questions.

1. Where were you yesterday? (I)   <u>I was at</u> _____ home.

2. Where were they yesterday? _____ zoo.

3. Where was he yesterday? _____ work.

4. Where were you yesterday? (We) _____ store.

5. Where were they last night? _____ movies.

6. Where was he yesterday? _____ church.

7. Where were you yesterday? (I) _____ school.

8. Where were they last night? _____ library.

9. Where was she last night? _____ work.

10. Where were you last night? (We) _____ laundromat.

11. Where was he last night? _____ home.

12. Where were you yesterday? (I) _____ park.

MAKE IT WORK

Answer the question. Tell about yourself.

■ I called you last Sunday, but you weren't at home. Where were you?

☐ _____

I WAS BORN ON JUNE 28.

Was Born and Were Born

I	was born	on June 28.
Singer Julio Iglesias	was born	on September 23.
Singers Julio Iglesias and Bruce Springsteen	were born	on September 23.

PRACTICE

Fill in the blanks with *was born* or *were born*.

1. Actor Mel Gibson and actress Victoria Principal <u>*were born*</u> on January 3.

2. Actor Burt Reynolds _____ on February 11.

3. Actress Elizabeth Taylor _____ on February 27.

4. Comedian Billy Crystal and Prince Albert of Monaco _____ on March 14.

5. Singer Liza Minnelli _____ on March 12.

6. Actress Glenn Close and actor Bruce Willis _____ on March 19.

7. Actor William Hurt _____ on March 20.

8. Comedian Eddie Murphy and actor Marlon Brando _____ on April 3.

9. Actress Joan Collins _____ on May 23.

10. Singer Michael Jackson _____ on August 29.

11. Singers Julio Iglesias and Bruce Springsteen _____ on September 23.

12. Soccer player Pélé and comedian Johnny Carson _____ on October 23.

13. Newscaster Dan Rather _____ on October 31.

14. Singer John Denver _____ on December 31.

MAKE IT WORK

Answer the questions. If necessary, see the Appendix for months.

When were you born? _____

Where were you born? _____

AKIRA AND I WERE BORN IN JUNE.

Prepositions of Time: *In* and *On*

Was Born and *Were Born*

I was born	on	June 28.
Akira and I were born	in	June.
Rafael and Louise were born	in	1955.

Note: Use *on* for dates: on June 28.
Use *in* for months and years: in 1955, in June.

PRACTICE

Fill in the blanks with *in* or *on*.

1. Actress Elizabeth Taylor was born __*in*__ 1932.

2. Tennis player Jimmy Connors was born _____ September 2.

3. Real estate developer Donald Trump and singer Paula Abdul were born _____ June.

4. Comedian Eddie Murphy was born _____ 1962.

5. Actor Tom Cruise was born _____ July 3.

6. Actor Al Pacino was born _____ 1940.

7. Baseball player Pete Rose and singer Glen Campbell were born _____ April.

8. Singer and actress Barbra Streisand was born _____ April 24.

9. Actress and singer Cher was born _____ 1946.

10. Actor Bruce Willis was born _____ March 19.

11. Actor Dustin Hoffman was born _____ 1938.

12. Comedian Billy Crystal and singer Liza Minnelli were born _____ March.

MAKE IT WORK

Find a classmate who was born in the same month or year as you were.
Then write about yourself and your classmate.

_____

_____

I STAYED AT HOME LAST SATURDAY NIGHT.

Affirmative Statements

Past of Regular Verbs and the Irregular Verb *To Go*

I		
I		
She	**stayed**	at home last Saturday night.
He	**went**	to bed early last Saturday night.
They		

Note: Add *d* or *ed* to form the past tense: stay + ed = stayed.
                                                              dance + d = danced.

irregular past tense verb: go–went

PRACTICE

Fill in the blanks with the correct form of the verb.

1. (go) Chang _went_____ to bed early last Saturday night.

2. (work) Loi _____ late.

3. (watch) Rosa and her husband _____ TV.

4. (play) Bob and Florie _____ miniature golf.

5. (listen) Rafael _____ to music.

6. (go) John and Marie _____ to the movies.

7. (dance) Mohsen and his friends _____ until 11:00 last Saturday night.

8. (visit) Julia _____ friends.

9. (exercise) Gloria and Oscar _____ at a health club.

10. (stay/relax) Louise and Raymond _____ at home and _____ .

11. (go) Anna _____ to a party.

12. (play) Akira _____ video games.

MAKE IT WORK

Answer the question.

What did you do last Saturday night? _____

_____

New Words: miniature golf   video game

121

Affirmative Statements

Past of Regular Verbs, Past of _To Be_

Résumé

Diane Peterson
1120 Creek Drive
Los Angeles, California 90069
Telephone: (310) 555-5422

WORK EXPERIENCE

2/90–PRESENT	Cashier
	Economy Drugstore
	Los Angeles, California
2/76–2/90	Cashier
	Garden Café
	Los Angeles, California
1/73–12/75	Waitress
	Big Tree Restaurant
	Eugene, Oregon

EDUCATION

Golden State	Diploma, June, 1972
High School	
Los Angeles, California	Major: Math

❧ Diploma ❧

Diane Peterson
completed courses and
graduated from Golden State High School.

Note: 2/90 = February 1990

New Words: high school = a school including grades nine through twelve
diploma

SHE STUDIED MATH IN HIGH SCHOOL.

> She | studied | math in high school.
>
> Note: For verbs ending in a consonant + *y*, drop the *y* and add *ied*.
>
> study = stud~~y~~ ied
>
> apply = appl~~y~~ ied
>
> For verbs ending in a vowel + *y*, add *ed*.
>
> enjoy = enjoyed
>
> play = played
>
> irregular past tense verb: is/are was/were

PRACTICE

Fill in the blanks with the correct form of the verb.

1. (attended) Diane Peterson ___attended___ Golden State High School.

2. (graduate) She _____ from high school in 1972.

3. (study) She _____ math in high school.

4. (be) At first, she _____ a waitress.

5. (work) She _____ at Big Tree Restaurant.

6. (start) She _____ her job in 1973.

7. (live) She _____ in Eugene, Oregon.

8. (move) In 1976, she _____ back to California.

9. (work) She _____ at Garden Café.

10. (be) She _____ a cashier.

11. (stay) She _____ at that job for 14 years.

12. (change) In 1990, she _____ jobs.

Now she works for Economy Drugstore.

MAKE IT WORK

Tell about your education and work experience.

_____

_____

At first, _____

Now _____

DID SHE SIGN THE APPLICATION? NO, SHE DIDN'T.

Negative and Affirmative Short Answers

Past of Regular Verbs

APPLICATION

Please use a pen.

Please print.

1. _Peterson_____ _Diane_____
   Last name   First   Middle

2. _1120 Creek Drive_____ _LosAngeles_____ _California_____
   Address   City   State   Zip Code

3. Telephone number _____ _555-5422_____
                             Area Code

4. Country of   a) _USA_____   b) _____
                       Birth   Citizenship

5. Date of Birth: _Oct._____ _27_____ _1954_____
                     Month   Day   Year

6. Check one:

   Sex: ❑ Male   ☑ Female

7. Check one:

             ❑ Married   ❑ Single

8. Do you have any physical disability or health problem?

   a)   ❑ Yes   ❑ No

   b) If yes, please explain: _____

9. In case of emergency, please contact:

   Name _____ _Dorothy Peterson_____

   Relation: ___ _Mother_____

   Address: ___ _Los Angeles, California 90969__

   Telephone: _(310) 555-6784_____

_____   _____

Signature of Applicant   Date

DID SHE SIGN THE APPLICATION? NO, SHE DIDN'T.

Did she fill in her last name?	Yes, she did.
Did she fill in her middle name?	No, she didn't.
Contraction: didn't = did not	

PRACTICE

Look at the application on page 124. Then answer the questions with short answers.

1. Did she answer all the questions on the application? _No, she didn't._____

2. Did she fill in her first name? _____

3. Did she fill in her middle name? _____

4. Did she write her telephone number? _____

5. Did she write her area code? _____

6. Did she fill in number 4a? _____

7. Did she fill in her date of birth? _____

8. Did she answer number 8? _____

9. Did she write her mother's address? _____

10. Did she write her mother's telephone number? _____

11. Did she sign the application? _____

12. Did she fill in the date? _____

MAKE IT WORK

Write your name and address. Then answer the questions.

Name: _____

Address: _____

Did you write your last name first? _____

Did you write your address, city, and state? _____

Did you write your zip code? _____

SHE DIDN'T USE A PEN.

Negative Statements

Past of Regular Verbs

She		used a pencil.
She	didn't use	a pen.

PRACTICE

Make negative sentences.

1. She used a pen.   *She didn't use a pen.* _____

2. She printed. _____

3. She filled in her middle name. _____

4. She filled in her zip code. _____

5. She checked a box for _____
   number 7. _____

6. She answered question _____
   number 8a. _____

7. She completed number 8b. _____

8. She filled in her mother's _____
   address. _____

9. She signed the application. _____

10. She answered all the _____
    questions. _____

MAKE IT WORK

Sign your name. Then make negative or affirmative sentences about your signature.

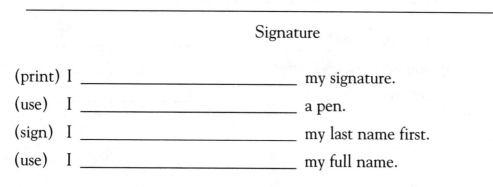

_____

Signature

(print) I _____ my signature.

(use)   I _____ a pen.

(sign)   I _____ my last name first.

(use)   I _____ my full name.

HE DIDN'T LIVE WITH HIS UNCLE. HE LIVED WITH HIS BROTHER.

Negative and Affirmative Statements

Past of Regular Verbs, Simple Present

He	didn't live	with his uncle.
He	lived	with his brother.

PRACTICE

Read the story. Then correct the sentences below. Write a negative sentence and an affirmative sentence. Use contractions whenever possible.

> Loi Van Ha was born in Vietnam in 1970. He started school when he was seven. He arrived in the United States when he was 13. At first he lived with his brother in Los Angeles. He attended high school in Los Angeles, and he worked in a gas station after school in the afternoon. He graduated from high school in 1990. After he graduated from high school, he studied auto mechanics at night. Then he changed jobs. Now he is a mechanic. He works at Quality Garage in Los Angeles. He lives in an apartment in Garden Grove.

1. Loi was born in China.   *He wasn't born in China.*

    He was born in Vietnam.

2. He arrived in the United

    States when he was seven. _____

    _____

    _____

3. He lived with his uncle. _____

    _____

4. He attended high school

    in San Francisco. _____

    _____

    _____

5. He worked in a factory
    in the afternoon after school. _____

    _____

    _____

6. He graduated from high
    school in 1970. _____

    _____

    _____

7. He studied accounting at night. _____

    _____

    _____

8. Now he's an accountant. _____

    _____

9. He works in a factory. _____

    _____

10. He lives in Los Angeles. _____

    _____

MAKE IT WORK

Tell about yourself.

I was born _____

I started school _____

_____

_____

_____

_____

WHEN DID YOU ARRIVE IN THE UNITED STATES?

Questions with *When, Where, Who, What*

Past of Regular Verbs, Past of *To Be*, Simple Present

| When did | you | arrive | in the United States? |

   I   arrived in the United States two years ago.

PRACTICE

Look at the chart. Write some questions you would like to ask a classmate.

			born?
			start school?
What			arrive in the United States?
Where	were	you	live with at first?
When	did		attend high school?
Who	do		graduate from high school?
			study in school?
			do now?
			work now?
			live now?

1. *Where were you born?* _____

2. _____

3. _____

4. _____

5. _____

6. _____

7. _____

8. _____

9. _____

10. _____

MAKE IT WORK

Correct Mohsen's English. Then rewrite the dialogue.

■ Mohsen: Where you attended high school, Loi?

☐ Loi: In Los Angeles.

■ Mohsen: _____

_____

☐ Loi: In Los Angeles.

129

HOW LONG DID HE WORK FOR NATIONAL BANK?

Questions with *When* and *How Long*

Past of Regular Verbs

	He worked	for ABC Company.
When	did he work	for ABC Company?
How long	did he work	for ABC Company?

PRACTICE

Make questions with *when* and *how long*.

He worked for ABC Company.　1. *When did he work for ABC Company?*

　　　　　　　　　　　　　　　2. *How long did he work for ABC Company?*

I lived in New York.　　　　　3. _____

　　　　　　　　　　　　　　　4. _____

She studied in France.　　　　5. _____

　　　　　　　　　　　　　　　6. _____

They worked in a hospital.　　7. _____

　　　　　　　　　　　　　　　8. _____

He worked for National Bank.　9. _____

　　　　　　　　　　　　　　　10. _____

We lived in England.　　　　　11. _____

　　　　　　　　　　　　　　　12. _____

I worked as a sales clerk.　　　13. _____

　　　　　　　　　　　　　　　14. _____

She attended college.　　　　　15. _____

　　　　　　　　　　　　　　　16. _____

They studied English.　　　　　17. _____

　　　　　　　　　　　　　　　18. _____

We lived in Texas.　　　　　　19. _____

　　　　　　　　　　　　　　　20. _____

Review: Past, Past of *To Be*

Mohsen	does	all the things he	enjoys	every Saturday.
Mohsen	did	all the things he	enjoyed	last Saturday.

irregular past tense verbs:	present	past
	go	went
	does/do	did
	is/are	was/were

PRACTICE

Read the sentences below. Then rewrite them. Tell what Mohsen did last Saturday. Change *go* to *went* and *doesn't* to *didn't*.

> Mohsen does all the things he enjoys every Saturday. It's his day off. In the morning, he doesn't get up until noon. In the afternoon, he plays tennis. In the evening, he cooks all of his favorite foods, and he invites his friends to dinner at his house. After dinner, Mohsen and his friends go to a dance at The Red Carpet. They stay there until 11:00 p.m. At 11:30, Mohsen watches The Late Show on TV. Finally, at 12:30, he goes to bed.

Mohsen did all the things he enjoyed last Saturday.

_____

_____

_____

_____

_____

_____

_____

_____

_____

_____

_____

YESTERDAY HE WAS IN MIAMI. TOMORROW HE'S GOING TO FLY TO CHICAGO.

Contrast: Past, Present Continuous, Future with *Going To*

Tonight the president	**is**	in New York.
Yesterday he	**was**	in Miami.
Tomorrow he's	**going to be**	in Chicago.

PRACTICE

Fill in the blanks with the correct tense, using contractions whenever possible. Read the entire news report before you begin.

Good evening. I'm Connie Rivera, and this is the evening news. Tonight the president _'s going to be_ (1. be) in New York. Right now, he _____ (2. meet) is with the mayor of New York. Yesterday, he _____ (3. be) in Miami. He _____ (4. talk) to the mayor of Miami. Tomorrow he _____ (5. fly) to Chicago. He _____ (6. talk) to the mayor of Chicago next Monday.

Singer Tomás Tomás _____ (7. die) last night at his home in Los Angeles. He _____ (8. be) 82. He _____ (9. be) born in Spain, and later he _____ (10. live) in the United States. In 1980, he _____ (11. have) six records on the "Top Ten" chart. And movie actress Lena Little and actor Dick Stone are engaged. They _____ (12. get) married next month.

In tennis last night, Henry Waterson _____ (13. play) Mike Wong. Waterson _____ (14. be) the winner, 6–4, 6–4, 6–2. Tomorrow Waterson _____ (15 play) José Garcia from Mexico.

YESTERDAY HE WAS IN MIAMI. TOMORROW HE'S GOING TO FLY TO CHICAGO.

The weather yesterday _____ cloudy and cool. It
(16. be)

_____ in Chicago yesterday. Right now the temperature
(17. rain)

_____ 64 degrees, and it _____ now. Tomorrow the
(18. be)   (19. rain)

rain _____ in Chicago. The temperature for the next few days
(20. continue)

_____ cool with a low of 58 degrees.
(21 be)

I'm Connie Rivera reporting for Channel 30. Good night.

MAKE IT WORK

Answer the questions about the news report.

Where is the president tonight?

_____

Who died last night?

_____

Who's going to get married?

_____

Who did Henry Waterson play last night?

_____

What's the weather going to be like in Chicago tomorrow?

_____

New Words: mayor = leader of a city or town
engaged = promised to be married
die = stop living

133

WE'RE STAYING AT THE EXCELSIOR HOTEL.

Contrast: Past, Present Continuous, Future with *Going To*

We	're	staying	at the Excelsior Hotel.
We		stayed	at the Excelsior Hotel last year.
We	're going to stay		at the Excelsior Hotel next year.

PRACTICE

Fill in the blanks with the correct tense using contractions whenever possible. Read the entire letter before you begin.

Dear Mom and Dad,

We're in New York now. There is so much to see. We're exhausted, but we <u>'re having</u> a wonderful time. Right now Bruce
___1. have___

_____, and I _____ this letter to you.
___2. sleep___   ___3. write___

We _____ at a hotel near Fifth Avenue. Yesterday
___4. stay___

we _____ along Fifth Avenue and _____ at
___5. walk___   ___6. look___

all the beautiful stores. We also _____ the World Trade
___7. visit___

Center yesterday. Tonight we _____ dinner at the Russian
___8. eat___

Tea Room. Tomorrow we _____ a bus tour of the city. On
___9. take___

Friday, we _____ the Statue of Liberty.
___10. see___

Wish you were here.

Love,
Susan

MAKE IT WORK

Answer the questions.

What city did you visit on your last vacation? _____

_____

What city are you going to visit on your next vacation? _____

_____

134

APPENDIX

Numbers

0 - zero	21 - twenty-one
1 - one	22 - twenty-two
2 - two	30 - thirty
3 - three	31 - thirty-one
4 - four	40 - forty
5 - five	50 - fifty
6 - six	60 - sixty
7 - seven	70 - seventy
8 - eight	80 - eighty
9 - nine	90 - ninety
10 - ten	100 - one hundred
11 - eleven	151 - one hundred fifty-one
12 - twelve	200 - two hundred
13 - thirteen	300 - three hundred
14 - fourteen	400 - four hundred
15 - fifteen	500 - five hundred
16 - sixteen	600 - six hundred
17 - seventeen	700 - seven hundred
18 - eighteen	800 - eight hundred
19 - nineteen	900 - nine hundred
20 - twenty	1,000 - one thousand

Days of the Week

Sunday
Monday
Tuesday
Wednesday
Thursday
Friday
Saturday

Months of the Year

January	July
February	August
March	September
April	October
May	November
June	December

ANSWERS TO EXERCISES

Page 1
2. 's
3. 're
4. 's
5. 'm
6. 're
7. 's
8. 's
9. 're
10. 'm
11. 's
12. 're

Page 2
2. She's from Greece.
3. He's from Colombia.
4. He's from Italy.
5. She's from Canada.
6. She's from France.
7. He's from Egypt.
8. He's from Japan.
9. She's from Brazil.
10. He's from China.

Page 3
2. Her middle name is Helen.
3. Her last name is Peterson.
4. His last name is Peterson.
5. His first name is Leonard.
6. Your first name is Brian.
7. Your last name is Burns.
8. His first name is John.
9. His last name is Burns.
10. His middle name is Christopher.
11. Her last name is Burns.
12. Her first name is Barbara.

Page 4 & 5
2. Susan's (or Diane's)
3. Dorothy's (or Leonard's)
4. Leonard's (or Dorothy's)
5. Susan's
6. Bruce's
7. Susan's
8. Susan's (or Bruce's)
9. Susan's (or Bruce's)
10. John's (or Brian's)
11. Brian's (or John's)
12. Barbara's (or Brian's)
13. John's (or Brian's or Barbara's)
14. John's (or Brian's or Barbara's)
15. John's (or Brian's or Barbara's)

Pages 6 & 7
2. He's heavy.
3. He's old (middle-aged).
4. It's short.
5. It's straight.
6. She's thin.
7. She's tall.
8. It's long.
9. It's curly.
10. He's young.
11. He's heavy.
12. He's short.

Pages 8 & 9
2. a
3. an
4. a
5. an
6. a
7. a
8. a
9. an
10. a
11. a
12. an
13. a
14. an
15. an
16. a
17. a
18. an
19. a
20. a

Page 10
2. She's a bad waitress.
3. She's a busy hairdresser.
4. He's a good teacher.
5. She's a hardworking nurse.
6. He's a lazy mechanic.
7. She's a busy secretary.
8. He's a bad manager.
9. She's a famous lawyer.
10. He's a hardworking salesperson.
11. She's a friendly receptionist.
12. He's a famous doctor.

Page 11
2. It's an easy job.
3. It's a difficult job.
4. It's an important job.
5. It's an interesting job.
6. It's a tiring job.
7. It's a boring occupation.
8. It's an exciting occupation.
9. It's a dangerous occupation.
10. It's an excellent occupation.
11. It's a terrible occupation.
12. It's a stressful occupation.

Page 12
Individual answers. Some possible answers are:
2. New York is an expensive city.
3. Los Angeles is a modern city.
4. London is a famous city.
5. Paris is a beautiful city.
6. Rome is an important city.
7. Madrid is an interesting city.
8. Mexico City is an exciting city.

Page 13
Her maiden name is Blanco. She's married, and her last name is Sánchez. Her husband is a dentist. Her father is an accountant, and her mother is a housewife. She's an interior decorator. She's also an ESL student. She's from Madrid.

Page 14
2. is, is
3. are
4. am, is
5. are
6. are, is
7. are
8. is, is
9. are
10. is, is
11. are
12. is, are

Page 15
2. They're Chinese.
3. We're Japanese.
4. She's Brazilian.
5. We're Egyptian.
6. He's Italian.
7. They're Canadian.
8. She's Mexican.
9. He's Colombian.
10. She's English.
11. We're French.

12. He's American.
13. They're Spanish.
14. They're Greek.

Page 16

2. His native language is Vietnamese.
3. Your native language is Spanish.
4. Her native language is Spanish.
5. His native language is Spanish.
6. Our native language is English.
7. My native language is English.
8. Your native language is Italian.
9. Their native language is French.
10. My native language is French.
11. Our native language is Japanese.
12. Her native language is Greek.

Page 17

2. They're cashiers.
3. They're managers.
4. They're lawyers.
5. They're ushers.
6. They're artists.
7. They're nurses.
8. They're doctors.
9. They're hairdressers.
10. They're engineers.
11. They're teachers.
12. They're dentists.

Make It Work.

He's a doctor. She's a doctor.
Possible answer:
They're doctors.

Page 18

2. They're interesting occupations.
3. We're experienced engineers.
4. They're difficult jobs.
5. You're busy receptionists.
6. They're bad waiters.
7. We're good cashiers.
8. You're excellent hairdressers.
9. They're important jobs.
10. They're famous actors.

11. They're intelligent students.
12. They're stressful jobs.

Make It Work.

Tom Cruise and Kevin Costner are good (famous/excellent) actors.

Page 19

2. Are you good accountants?
3. Is he a good cashier?
4. Is she a good hairdresser?
5. Are you a good secretary?
6. Is she a good nurse?
7. Are they good lawyers?
8. Are you good electricians?
9. Is he a good mechanic?
10. Are you good doctors?
11. Are they good dentists?
12. Are you a good interior decorator?

Make It Work.

Is she a good hairdresser?

Page 20

2. Is he from
3. Is she from
4. Are they from
5. Is she from
6. Is he from
7. Are they from
8. Is she from
9. Are they from
10. Is she from
11. Are they from
12. Is she from

Make It Work

Oh. Are you from Tokyo?

Page 21

2. No. She isn't here right now.
3. No. They aren't here right now.
4. No. She isn't here right now.
5. No. They aren't here right now.
6. No. He isn't here right now.
7. No. They aren't here right now.
8. No. They aren't here right now.
9. No. She isn't here right now.
10. No. He isn't here right now.

Make It Work.

No. She isn't here right now.
No. I'm sorry. Her husband isn't here right now either.

Page 22

2. aren't
3. is
4. are
5. is
6. isn't
7. isn't
8. is
9. aren't
10. are

Pages 23 & 24

2. Yes, he is.
3. No, he isn't.
4. No, you aren't.
5. Yes, you are.
6. Yes, you are.
7. No, they aren't.
8. Yes, they are.
9. No, he isn't.
10. Yes, she is.
11. No, she isn't.
12. No, she isn't.
13. Yes, she is.
14. No, she isn't.
15. No, she isn't.
16. Yes, they are.
17. Yes, he is.
18. No, she isn't.
19. Yes, they are.
20. No, they aren't.
21. No, she isn't.
22. Yes, he is.

Make It Work.

Individual answers. Possible answers are:
No, I'm not.
Yes, I am.

Page 25

2. My name is Marie Du Lac.
3. Are your from the United States?
4. No, I'm not. I am from Canada.
5. Are you from Montreal?
6. No, I'm not. I am from Quebec?
7. Quebec is a beautiful city. Are you French?
8. I am Canadian. My native language is French.
9. Are you American?
10. Yes, I am. I'm from Los Angeles.

137

Pages 26 & 27

2. It's eight ten.
3. It's one twenty.
4. It's five thirty.
5. It's nine fifty.
6. It's three forty-five.
7. It's four fifteen.
8. It's eleven o'clock.
9. It's six thirty-five.
10. It's twelve thirty.

Page 28

2. He's never late for work.
3. He's sometimes early.
4. At his office, he's usually busy.
5. He's often tired, too.
6. But he's rarely angry.
7. He's usually nice to his patients.
8. His patients are sometimes nervous.
9. But Dr. Lau is never nervous.
10. He's always friendly to everyone.

Page 29

2. Fifteen and 76/100—
3. Thirty-nine and 95/100—
4. Nineteen and 99/100—
5. Forty-five and No/100—
6. Fifty and 80/100—
7. Ninety-two and 75/100—
8. Sixty-three and 54/100—
9. Eighty-eight and 99/100—
10. Seventy-four and No/100—

Make It Work.

Twenty-eight and 07/100—

Pages 30 & 31

2. forks
3. napkins
4. dishes
5. pans
6. glasses
7. cups
8. plates
9. hairbrushes
10. trays
11. chairs
12. couches
13. toasters
14. jewelry boxes
15. blankets
16. clocks
17. watches
18. purses
19. dresses
20. shirts

Page 32

2. peaches
3. strawberries
4. bananas
5. cherries
6. oranges
7. tomatoes
8. radishes
9. carrots
10. potatoes

Page 33

2. women
3. ladies
4. boys
5. construction workers
6. children
7. babies
8. nurses
9. girls
10. waitresses

Make It Work.

shoes for women (ladies)

Page 34

2. That's
3. This is
4. This is
5. That's
6. That's
7. This is
8. That's

Page 35

2. Are these your credit cards?
3. Are those your books?
4. Are these your pens?
5. Are these your glasses?
6. Are those your keys?

Make It Work.

Are these your gloves?

Page 36

2. That tie is on sale.
3. Those slacks are on sale.
4. That jacket is on sale.
5. Those shoes are on sale.
6. Those jeans are on sale.
7. That blouse is on sale.
8. That skirt is on sale.
9. Those boots are on sale.
10. Those socks are on sale.

Page 37

2. Those jackets are nice.
3. These T-shirts are great.
4. These wallets are pretty.
5. Those purses are nice.
6. Those sweaters are beautiful.
7. Those ties are pretty.
8. These coats are ugly.
9. Those shirts are nice.
10. Those blouses are pretty.
11. These dresses are beautiful.
12. These hats are great.

Make It Work.

Possible answers:

Those gloves are pretty.
(beautiful, nice)
Those shoes are nice.
(beautiful)

Page 38

2. How much is it?
3. How much is it?
4. How much are they?
5. How much are they?
6. How much is it?
7. How much are they?
8. How much are they?
9. How much is it?
10. How much is it?
11. How much are they?
12. How much is it?

Make It Work.

How much are they?
How much is it?
How much are they?

Page 39

2. Who
3. Where
4. What time
5. Who
6. What time
7. Where
8. What class
9. What class
10. Who
11. What time
12. Who
13. What class
14. Where

Page 40

2. Where is his class?
3. What time is his class?
4. Who is his teacher?
5. What class is he in?
6. Who is his teacher?
7. What time is his class?
8. Where is his class?
9. What class is she in?
10. Who is her instructor (teacher)?
11. Where is her class?
12. What time is her class?

Page 41
Individual answers.

Page 42

2. 'm
3. are
4. 're
5. is
6. 'm
7. is
8. is
9. 're
10. is
11. is
12. 's
13. are
14. is
15. is
16. 're
17. is
18. 's

Page 43

2. on
3. in
4. on
5. in
6. on
7. in
8. in
9. on
10. in
11. in
12. in
13. on
14. in

Make It Work.
on

Pages 44 & 45

2. There's
3. There's
4. There are
5. There's
6. There's
7. There's
8. There are
9. There's
10. There's
11. There are
12. There's
13. There's
14. There's

Page 46

2. the
3. the
4. a
5. the
6. a
7. the
8. a
9. the
10. a
11. the
12. a
13. a
14. a

Make It Work.
Is there a dishwasher in the kitchen?
Yes. The dishwasher is right over there.

Page 47

2. Is there a dishwasher in the kitchen?
3. Are there counters in the kitchen?
4. Are there electrical outlets in the kitchen?
5. Is there a window in the kitchen?
6. Is there a washing machine in the kitchen?
7. Are there cabinets in the kitchen?
8. Is there a shower in the bathroom?
9. Are there tiles in the bathroom?
10. Is there a bathtub in the bathroom?
11. Are there windows in the living room?
12. Is there a fireplace in the living room?

Page 48

2. Is there a lock on the door?
3. Are there lights in the hallways?
4. Is there a washing machine in the building?
5. Is there a stove in the kitchen?
6. Are there closets in the apartment?
7. Is there a fire detector in the apartment?
8. Are there electrical outlets in the apartment?
9. Are there windows in the apartment?
10. Is there a shower in the bathroom?

Page 49

2. Yes, there is.
3. No, there aren't.
4. Yes, there is.
5. No, there isn't.
6. Yes, there are.
7. Yes, there are.
8. No, there isn't.
9. Yes, there are.
10. Yes, there is.
11. No, there aren't.
12. No, there isn't.

Pages 50 & 51

2. There are some
3. There are some
4. There are some
5. There's some
6. There are some
7. There's some
8. There are some
9. There's some
10. There's some
11. There are some
12. There's some
13. There are some
14. There's some
15. There are some
16. There are some
17. There are some
18. There's some
19. There are some
20. There's some

Page 52

3. a
4. a
5. a

6. a
7. some
8. some
9. some
10. a
11. some
12. a
13. a
14. some

Page 53

3. There aren't any glasses on the table.
4. There aren't any napkins on the table.
5. There isn't any meat on the table.
6. There isn't any water on the table.
7. There aren't any vegetables on the table.
8. There isn't any bread on the table.
9. There isn't any soda on the table.
10. There isn't any pepper on the table.
11. There isn't any salt on the table.
12. There aren't any cups on the table.
13. There isn't any coffee on the table.
14. There aren't any spoons on the table.

Page 54

singular countable nouns:
a tomato
a cucumber
plural countable nouns:
French fries
carrots
strawberries
uncountable nouns:
ice cream
orange juice
lettuce
margarine
mayonnaise

Page 55

3. There's a lemon in the refrigerator.
4. There are some carrots in the refrigerator.
5. There's some milk in the refrigerator.
6. There isn't any cream in the refrigerator.
7. There's a tomato in the refrigerator.
8. There are some strawberries in the refrigerator.
9. There isn't any soda in the refrigerator.
10. There aren't any apples in the refrigerator.
11. There's some mayonnaise in the refrigerator.
12. There's a cucumber in the refrigerator.
13. There are some eggs in the refrigerator.
14. There isn't any coffee in the refrigerator.
15. There aren't any oranges in the refrigerator.
16. There's some orange juice in the refrigerator.

Page 56

2. Is there any soda?
3. Are there any tomatoes?
4. Is there any rice?
5. Is there any milk?
6. Are there any eggs?
7. Are there any napkins?
8. Is there any bread?
9. Is there any coffee?
10. Are there any potatoes?
11. Is there any margarine?
12. Are there any carrots?

Make It Work.
Is there any ice cream?
Are there any strawberries?

Page 57

Individual answers.
Some possible answers are
2. There's a desk in the classroom.
3. There's a book on the desk.
4. There's a bookcase in the classroom.
5. There are some books in the bookcase.
6. There's a wastebasket in the classroom.
7. There are two windows in the classroom.
8. There's a chalkboard in the classroom.
9. There's a clock on the wall.
10. There's a map on the wall.

Pages 58 & 59

2. is eating
3. is reading
4. are playing
5. is sleeping
6. are talking
7. is taking
8. are flying
9. is playing
10. is looking
11. are listening
12. holding
13. is fishing

Page 60

2. 's wearing
3. 's wearing
4. 're carrying
5. 're looking
6. 's wearing
7. 's carrying
8. 's wearing
9. 're holding
10. 're wearing

Page 61

2. smiling
3. drinking
4. having
5. relaxing
6. watching
7. enjoying
8. working
9. standing
10. putting
11. setting
12. smiling
13. frowning
14. getting.

Make It Work.
She's standing.
She's sitting.

Page 62

2. aren't sitting down.
3. isn't drinking soda.
4. aren't drinking soda.
5. isn't relaxing.
6. aren't relaxing.
7. isn't watching television.

8. aren't watching television.
9. isn't smiling.
10. aren't smiling.
11. isn't enjoying the television program.
12. aren't enjoying the television program.
13. isn't having a good time.
14. aren't having a good time.

Page 63
2. She's wearing a skirt.
3. She isn't wearing a jacket.
4. She isn't wearing sneakers.
5. She's wearing a blouse.
6. She's wearing boots.
7. She's wearing a raincoat.
8. She isn't wearing a suit.
9. She isn't carrying (wearing) a briefcase.
10. She isn't wearing an umbrella. (She isn't holding/carrying an umbrella).
11. She isn't wearing a hat.
12. She's wearing a scarf.

Make It Work.
He isn't wearing slacks.
He's wearing a skirt.
He isn't wearing (any) shoes or socks.

Page 64
2. Is she setting the table?
3. Is she eating?
4. Is she getting dinner ready?
5. Is she washing the dishes?
6. Are they watching television?
7. Are they playing cards?
8. Are they listening to the radio?
9. Is she relaxing?
10. Is she sleeping?
11. Is she reading?
12. Is she talking on the telephone?
13. Are they talking?
14. Are they drinking soda?
15. Are they having a good time?

Page 65
2. Yes, they are.
3. No, they aren't.
4. Yes, they are.
5. No, they aren't.
6. Yes, they are.
7. No, he isn't.
8. Yes, she is.

9. No, he isn't.
10. Yes, she is.
11. No, he isn't.
12. Yes, she is.
Make It Work.
Individual answers.
Possible answers are:
Yes, I am.
No, I'm not.

Page 66
2. What's he reading?
   A book.
3. What are they doing?
   They're cooking.
4. What are they cooking?
   Eggs
5. What are they doing?
   They're eating.
6. What are they eating?
   Ice cream cones.
7. What's she doing?
   She's writing.
8. What's she writing?
   A check.

Page 67
2. It's snowing in Montreal.
3. It's windy in Madrid.
4. It's cloudy in Los Angeles.
5. It's raining in London.
6. It's sunny in Athens.
7. It's cloudy in Tokyo.
8. It's snowing in New York.
9. It's raining in Paris.
10. It's sunny in Mexico City.

Page 68
Individual answers:
Some possible answers are:
2. In Mexico City, people are probably getting up.
3. In Bogotá, people are probably eating.
4. In Rio de Janeiro, people are probably working.
5. In London, people are probably eating lunch.
6. In Athens, people are probably working.
7. In Bombay, people are probably eating dinner.
8. In Manila, people are probably watching television.
9. In Tokyo, people are probably

getting ready for bed.
10. In Wellington, people are probably sleeping.

Page 69
2. They're going to play ping-pong (table tennis).
3. She's going to play golf.
4. They're going to play baseball.
5. They're going to play soccer.
6. They're going to play football.

Pages 70 & 71
2. is going to water the flowers.
3. is going to mow the lawn.
4. are going to wash the car.
5. are going to play tennis.
6. is going to ride her bicycle.
7. is going to swim.
8. are going to play baseball.
9. is going to play golf.
10. is going to sit in the sun.

Page 72
2. Yes, she is.
3. No, she isn't.
4. No, they aren't.
5. No, they aren't.
6. Yes, they are.
7. No, she isn't.
8. Yes, she is.
9. No, she isn't.
10. No, they aren't.
11. No, they aren't.
12. Yes, they are.

Page 73
2. isn't going to water the flowers.
3. isn't going to mow the lawn.
4. aren't going to wash the car.
5. aren't going to play tennis.
6. isn't going to ride her bicycle.
7. isn't going to swim.
8. aren't going to play baseball.
9. isn't going to play golf.
10. isn't going to sit in the sun.

Page 74
2. aren't going to run tomorrow.
3. isn't going to exercise tomorrow.
4. aren't going to exercise tomorrow.
5. isn't going to play soccer tomorrow.

6. aren't going to play soccer tomorrow.
7. isn't going to dance tomorrow.
8. aren't going to dance tomorrow.
9. isn't going to take a walk tomorrow.
10. aren't going to take a walk tomorrow.
11. isn't going to work tomorrow.
12. aren't going to work tomorrow.

Page 75

2. Who is she going to play ping-pong with?
3. What time is she going to play ping-pong?
4. When is she going to go to the movies?
5. Who is she going to go to the movies with?
6. What time is she going to go to the movies?
7. When is she going to have dinner (with Oscar and Gloria)?
8. Who is she going to have dinner with?
9. What time is she going to have dinner?
10. When is she going to go to Susan's party?
11. Who is she going to go to Susan's party with?
12. What time is she going to go to Susan's party?

Page 76

so they aren't going to have time to see everything. They're going to take a bus tour of the city. Then they're going to visit the World Trade Center. They're also going to see the Statue of Liberty, but they aren't going to climb the stairs to the top. They're going to eat at some famous restaurants, and they're going to shop on Fifth Avenue. They're going to take their camera. They're going to take a lot of pictures.

Page 77

2. 's holding
3. 's going to play

4. 's taking
5. 's listening
6. 's going to rain.
7. 're going to swim.
8. 're wearing
9. 's holding
10. 's going to take
11. 're carrying
12. 're standing

Page 78

2. are moving
3. is
4. 's raining
5. is
6. 's going to rain
7. 's going to be
8. 's going to be
9. 's going to get
10. 's going to be
11. 's going to snow.
12. 're going to need

Page 79

2. across from
3. next to
4. across from
5. between
6. next to
7. between
8. next to
9. on
10. across from
11. next to
12. on

Page 80

A. The hospital is on the corner, approximately one block from the hospital sign.
B. Individual answers.
One possible answer is:
2. Turn left.
3. Go two blocks.
4. Turn left.
5. Go two blocks.
6. Look for the sign.
7. The bus stop is on the corner.

Page 81

2. Don't turn left.
3. Don't walk.
4. Don't turn around.
5. Don't turn right.
6. Don't drive in the right lane.

7. Don't stop here.

Page 82
2. I work
3. They work
4. He works
5. We work
6. You work
7. She works
8. I work
9. We work
10. They work
11. They work
12. She works

Page 83
2. stands
3. waits
4. likes
5. goes
6. plays
7. watches, tries
8. chases, catches
9. comes
10. drinks
11. sits, washes
12. goes
13. eats
14. relaxes, sleeps

Page 84
2. in
3. at
4. At
5. in
6. At
7. In
8. At
9. at
10. at
11. at
12. in
13. at
14. at

Page 85
2. He always exercises.
3. He often exercises for two hours.
4. For breakfast, he never drinks coffee.
5. He always drinks milk.
6. He rarely eats too much.
7. He never smokes cigarettes.
8. He never drinks wine.

9. He usually sleeps eight hours at night.
10. He sometimes sleeps nine or ten hours at night.

Page 86
2. She has a headache.
3. He has a toothache.
4. He has a backache.
5. I have an earache.
6. She has a sore throat.
7. I have a sore finger.
8. He has a fever.
9. I have a cough.
10. She has a cold.

Make It Work.
I have a headache.

Page 87
2. has
3. has
4. have
5. have
6. have
7. have
8. has
9. have
10. have

Pages 88 & 89
2. likes his job (at the bank).
3. lives in an apartment (two blocks from the bank).
4. walks to work.
5. goes to school.
6. also has a part-time job.
7. works in her parents' restaurant (at night).
8. lives with her parents (in a house).
9. is a construction worker.
10. He has four children (has a tough job).
11. works in a department store.
12. lives in a house with a big yard (because she has a lot of pets).
13. loves animals.
14. has four dogs and three cats.

Page 90
works in a hospital, and she takes care of her family. She gets up at 5:30 every morning. She cooks breakfast for her son and her

husband. At 6:30 she gets her son, Paco, ready for school. At 7:00 she drives Paco to school. She gets to the hospital at 7:30. She works from 7:30 to 3:30. After work she picks up Paco at school. She goes home, and she cooks dinner. After dinner she does the dishes. On Wednesday evening, she goes to class. After class, she makes lunch for her husband and her son. She sometimes watches television in the evening if she's not too tired. She usually goes to bed at 10:30.

Page 91
Individual questions
Some possible questions are:
2. Do you like your job?
3. Do you go to school?
4. Does your husband (or wife) work?
5. Do you have any children?
6. Do your children live with you?
7. Do your children go to school?
8. Do you have any brothers and sisters?
9. Does your brother (or sister) live with you?
10. Do you have any pets?

Page 92
3. Do they live in Los Angeles?
4. Do they do the same thing every evening?
5. Do they get up at 9:00 at night?
6. Do they go to work at 10:00?
7. Do they work from 11:00 to 7:00?
8. Do they come home from work in the morning?
9. Does Mr. Gross go to bed at 1:00 p.m.?
10. Does Mr. Tong go to bed at 2:00?
11. Is Mr. Tong a night watchman?
12. Does he watch buildings at night?
13. Does he work for a construction company?
14. Is Mr. Gross a night watch-man, too?
15. Does he work for a movie

studio?

Page 93

3. Yes, they do.
4. No, they don't.
5. Yes, they do.
6. No, they don't.
7. Yes, they do.
8. No, they don't.
9. Yes, he is.
10. Yes, he does.
11. No, he doesn't
12. Yes, he does.
13. Yes, he is.
14. Yes, he does.
15. No, he doesn't.

Page 94

2. They don't have breakfast in the morning.
3. The don't go to work at 8:00.
4. They don't get to work at 9:00.
5. They don't work from 9:00 to 5:00.
6. They don't come home in the evening.
7. Mr. Tong doesn't eat dinner in the evening.
8. He doesn't relax at night.
9. He doesn't watch television.
10. He doesn't go to bed at 11:00 at night.
11. Mr. Gross doesn't read at night.
12. He doesn't go to bed at midnight.
13. Mr. Tong and Mr. Gross don't sleep at night.
14. They don't work in the daytime.
15. Night watchmen don't watch buildings in the daytime.

Page 95

doesn't make a lot of money. She and her husband don't live in a big house in Beverly Hills. They don't have a private movie theater in their house. Marie doesn't drive a Rolls Royce. She doesn't wear expensive clothes. She doesn't have a lot of beautiful jewelry. She and her husband don't give a lot of big parties. They don't own an airplane. They don't travel to Spain for their vacations. Marie doesn't have it all.

Page 96

2. has them.
3. have it.
4. has it.
5. have them.
6. has it.
7. have it.
8. has them.
9. have it.
10. has it.
11. have them.
12. has it.

Make It Work.

them. They

Page 97

2. them
3. us
4. her
5. me
6. him
7. them
8. us
9. her
10. him
11. them
12. us

Make It Work.

Please help me.

Page 98

2. I don't know him.
3. she doesn't know us.
4. he doesn't see you.
5. we don't see them.
6. they don't see us.
7. I don't hear her.
8. you don't hear me.
9. I don't hear him.
10. he doesn't understand me.
11. you don't understand them.
12. we don't understand you.

Make It Work.

He, her, she, him.

Page 99

2. in
3. at
4. in
5. at
6. on
7. in
8. on
9. at
10. in
11. at
12. on

13. in
14. on
15. at
16. in

Page 100

2. Where on Flower Street does he live?
3. Where in Hollywood does he work?
4. Where on Doheny Drive does he work?
5. Where in New York do they live?
6. Where on Park Avenue do they live?
7. Where in San Francisco do you work?
8. Where on Market Street do you work?
9. Where in Miami Beach does she live?
10. Where on Atlantic Road does she live?
11. Where in Chicago do you work?
12. Where on Lakeshore Drive do you work?

Make It Work.

Where do you work?
Where on Park Avenue do you work?

Page 101

2. Where does he work?
   He works in New York (on Fifth Avenue/at 500 Fifth Avenue).
3. What company does he work for?
   He works for Turner and Turner.
4. What does she do?
   She's an interior decorator.
5. Where does she work?
   She works in Los Angeles (on Sunset Boulevard/at 5116 Sunset Boulevard).
6. What company does she work for?
   She works for Home Interiors.
7. What do they do?
   They're doctors.
8. Where do they work?
   They work in Chicago. (on Lake

144

Drive/at 2400 Lake Drive).

9. What company do they work
   for?
   They work for J.G.S. Medical
   Group.

Page 102

2. work
3. takes
4. 's (is)
5. is
6. wakes
7. eats
8. reads
9. takes
10. drinks
11. gets
12. has
13. go
14. takes
15. eats
16. get
17. have
18. play
19. watch
20. goes
21. are
22. go

Page 103

2. works
3. works
4. 're relaxing
5. 're playing
6. play
7. watch
8. 're watching
9. watches
10. 's sleeping
11. falls
12. is playing
13. goes
14. go

Page 104

2. It never snows in the summer.
3. It sometimes rains in the
   summer.
4. It's usually cool in the fall.
5. It sometimes rains in the fall.
6. It usually snows in the winter.
7. It's always cold in the winter.
8. It usually rains a lot in the
   spring.
9. It's often warm in the spring.
10. It rarely snows in the spring.

Page 105

2. are wearing
3. rains
4. wear
5. 's snowing
6. are wearing
7. snows
8. wear
9. 's
10. are wearing
11. wear
12. 's
13. are wearing
14. wear
15. wear

Page 106

2. In fact, they can ski very well.
3. In fact, she can ice-skate very
   well.
4. In fact, she can ride a bicycle
   very well.
5. In fact, they can play golf
   very well.
6. In fact, he can play baseball
   very well.
7. In fact, she can play the
   piano very well.
8. In fact, they can dance very
   well.
9. In fact, he can play the guitar
   very well.
10. In fact, she can play tennis
    very well.
11. In fact, they can play chess
    very well.
12. In fact, he can cook very
    well.

Page 107

2. They can't cook.
3. She can't ski.
4. They can't swim.
5. He can't play the guitar.
6. She can't ride a bicycle.

Page 108

2. very
3. too
4. very
5. too
6. too
7. too
8. very

9. too
10. too
11. very
12. too

Make It Work.

His tie is too short.
His jacket is too small.
His slacks are too big (loose).

Page 109

2. She's very beautiful.
3. He's too short.
4. It's too expensive.
5. She's very happy.
6. He's very strong.

Pages 110 & 111

Individual answers are:
Yes, I can. No. I can't.

Page 112

2. Can you move it?
3. Can you lift them?
4. Can you open it?
5. Can you close it?
6. Can you carry them?
7. Can you reach it?
8. Can you lift them?
9. Can you find it?
10. Can you carry them?

Make It Work.

Can you lift 100 pounds?
Can you lift 40 pounds?

Page 113

Individual answers:
I can't draw.
I can draw but not very well. I can
draw very well.

Page 114

2. was
3. was
4. were
5. was
6. were
7. were
8. were
9. was
10. was
11. was
12. was

Page 115

2. The beaches weren't nice.
3. They weren't clean.

4. The bus tour wasn't interesting.
5. The city wasn't very pretty.
6. The restaurants weren't very good.
7. The people weren't friendly.
8. They weren't very helpful.
9. The weather wasn't nice.
10. It wasn't warm and sunny.
11. Marie's hotel wasn't large.
12. It wasn't new and modern.
13. It wasn't on the beach.
14. Her room wasn't very clean.

Page 116

2. Were they safe?
3. Were they crowded?
4. Were they expensive?
5. Was it sunny?
6. Was it warm?
7. Was it hot?
8. Were they helpful?
9. Were they friendly?
10. Was it modern?
11. Was it old?
12. Was it on the beach?
13. Was it near the beach?
14. Were they large?
15. Were they expensive
16. Was it interesting?

Page 117

2. Yes, he was.
3. No, she wasn't.
4. Yes, she was.
5. No, he wasn't.
6. Yes, he was.
7. No, she wasn't.
8. No, they weren't.
9. Yes, they were.
10. Yes, he was.
11. Yes, they were.
12. No, they weren't.

Page 118

2. They were at the
3. He was at
4. We were at the
5. They were at the
6. He was at
7. I was at
8. They were at the
9. She was at
10. We were at the
11. He was at
12. I was at the

Page 119

2. was born
3. was born
4. were born
5. was born
6. were born
7. was born
8. were born
9. was born
10. was born
11. were born
12. were born
13. was born
14. was born

Page 120

2. on
3. in
4. in
5. on
6. in
7. in
8. on
9. in
10. on
11. in
12. in

Page 121

2. worked
3. watched
4. played
5. listened
6. went
7. danced
8. visited
9. exercised
10. stayed, relaxed
11. went
12. played

Pages 122 & 123

2. graduated
3. studied
4. was
5. worked
6. started
7. lived
8. moved
9. worked
10. was
11. stayed
12. changed

Pages 124 & 125

2. Yes, she did.
3. No, she didn't.
4. Yes, she did.
5. No, she didn't.
6. Yes, she did.
7. Yes, she did.
8. No, she didn't.
9. No, she didn't.
10. Yes, she did.
11. No, she didn't.
12. No, she didn't.

Page 126

2. She didn't print.
3. She didn't fill in her middle name.
4. She didn't fill in her zip code.
5. She didn't check a box for number 7.
6. She didn't answer question number 8a.
7. She didn't complete number 8b.
8. She didn't fill in her mother's address.
9. She didn't sign the application.
10. She didn't answer all the questions.

Pages 127 & 128

2. He didn't arrive in the United States when he was seven. He arrived in the United States when he was 13.
3. He didn't live with his uncle. He lived with his brother.
4. He didn't attend high school in San Francisco. He attended high school in Los Angeles.
5. He didn't work in a factory after school in the afternoon. He worked in a gas station.
6. He didn't graduate from high school in 1970. He gradated (from high school) in 1990.
7. He didn't study accounting at night. He studied auto mechanics.
8. Now he isn't an accountant. He's a mechanic.
9. He doesn't work in a factory. He works at Quality Garage (in a garage).
10. He doesn't live in Los Angeles. He lives in Garden Grove.

Page 129

Individual questions. Some possible questions are:

2. When did you start school?
3. When did you arrive in the United States?
4. Who did you live with at first?
5. Where did you attend high school?
6. When did you graduate from high school?
7. What did you study in school?
8. What do you do now?
9. Where do you work now?
10. Where do you live now?

Make It Work.

Mohsen: Where did you attend high school. Loi?

Page 130

3. When did you live in New York?
4. How long did you live in New York?
5. When did she study in France?
6. How long did she study in France?
7. When did they work in a hospital?
8. How long did they work in a hospital?
9. When did he work for National Bank?
10. How long did he work for National Bank?
11. When did you live in England?
12. How long did you live in England?
13. When did you work as a sales clerk?
14. How long did you work as a sales clerk?
15. When did she attend college?
16. How long did she attend college?
17. When did they study English?
18. How long did they study English?
19. When did you live in Texas?
20. How long did you live in

Texas?

Page 131

It was his day off. In the morning, he didn't get up until noon. In the afternoon, he played tennis. In the evening, he cooked all of his favorite foods, and he invited his friends to dinner at his house. After dinner, Mohsen and his friends went to a dance at The Red Carpet. They stayed there until 11:00 P.M. At 11:30, Mohsen watched The Late Shown on TV. Finally, at 12:30, he went to bed.

Pages 132 & 133

2. 's meeting
3. was
4. talked
5. 's going to fly
6. 's going to talk
7. died
8. was
9. was
10. lived
11. had
12. 're going to get
13. played
14. was
15. is going to play
16. was
17. rained
18. is
19. 's raining
20. is going to continue
21. is going to be

Make It Work.

The president is in New York.
Singer Tomas Tomas died.
Movie actress Lena Little and actor Dick Stone are going to get married.
Henry Waterson played Mike Wong.
It's going to rain. It's going to be cool (58 degrees).